A Guide through Breaking Up without Heartbreak

A Guide through Breaking Up without Heartbreak

✦

Using the Laws of Nature to Learn How to Let Go with Love.

Christopher Walker

iUniverse, Inc.
New York   Bloomington

A Guide through Breaking Up without Heartbreak
Using the Laws of Nature to Learn How to Let Go with Love.

Edited by Helena Maria Rodriguez Walker

iUniverse books may be ordered through booksellers or by contacting:

iUniverse
1663 Liberty Drive
Bloomington, IN 47403
www.iuniverse.com
1-800-Authors (1-800-288-4677)

ISBN: 978-0-595-52580-5 (pbk)
ISBN: 978-0-595-62634-2 (ebk)

Printed in the United States of America

Contents

Introduction

In this book I apply ancient wisdom to modern times to help you let go and to move forward in your life with love and passion.

The ancient Laws of Nature tap the deepest core of your humanity, and deal with emotional attachments, heartbreak and complex human dynamics with accuracy, compassion and clarity. I think you will find this quite refreshing.

If you speak to most people who have gone through breaking up more than ten years in the past they'll begin to tell you how challenging it was at the time but how thankful they are now that it happened. They'll say things like, "I went through hell, but if it didn't happen, I wouldn't be here right now, with my new love and my new life". This is the wisdom of time and it demonstrates exactly what this book is going to give you. The wisdom of time, right now.

As the author, I have drawn on thousands of consultations I have done with people from all walks of life: Movie stars, rock stars, entrepreneurs, world leaders, artists, indigenous peoples and everyday families from most countries on earth and I can honestly say that the languages vary but the issues don't. People are really universal when it comes to break ups. The only difference is their wisdom and how they apply it.

The skills for letting go are an important part of life. Nothing is permanent, not even your own life. So, letting go applies to releasing relationships even when we don't want to, and it applies to letting go those we love as they pass this earth.

However, without doubt, the hardest process is for those whose letting go process is not voluntary. The subject of their attachment is still in their heart but unavailable for the possibility of a romance. Those who have no choice but to let go.

So, the Laws of Nature really can help. They give you the wisdom of hindsight before experience teaches it to you. They are predictive so they help you see the better path through the challenges of relationships and they neutralize the temptation to make bad decisions that can have long term, disastrous results.

Learn not to react during times of emotional challenge is an important part of the teachings of the Laws of Nature. Think like nature, know that the seasons of storms and disasters are just cycles, and that there are good times ahead, no matter what. Learning to let go is the key to both healthy relationships that you are in and the ones that need to move to a new place in your heart.

You can know that letting go of someone is a choice. It is a mind-game, one that you choose to enact when the pain of holding on is greater than the pain of letting go. What I aim to share with you here is the science of undertaking that journey of letting go, once you have made up your mind, once and for all, that it is time. You must know that nobody can make that one decision for you. It's yours, but once made, and a commitment to letting go is final, this book is an amazing guide.

The real hell is the no-mans-land between holding on and letting go. That stage of uncertainty when, either by delusion or through fear of the future, you just can't make up your mind. Really, if I can encourage you in any direction it is to take the time to make this decision well and make it final. The vacillation of going backward and forward is just going to ruin your life, degrade your health and get you involved in messy business. People don't change, even if they promise to, people don't change, and if you remember this, it will make the choices much clearer.

When I was training for the Australian Rowing Championships I had the good luck to share the river with some of the greatest oarsmen and women of their time. I tried to learn from them, and they were generous in sharing technique and tips. But the one thing they all achieved that was nearly impossible to emulate with a conventional mindset was their capacity to be cool under pressure.

I was always shocked at my own race psychology. About half way down that gruelling 2,000-meter straight-line course, my body would be praying for me to give up and every sense in my mind would join in that symphony, screaming, "STOP – it's not worth it." Each time I raced somehow I'd get through that terrible nightmare of pain and emotional agony, and then, at the 200 meter to go peg, I find a whole new bundle of energy. What became apparent was that this middle time in the race was not real, I did have plenty in reserve, and I proved that over and over again by sprinting to the finish. It was all a huge mind game.

Those champions had mastered the mind over emotion equation. They could go through a physical hell and yet; the look on their face was relaxed and calm. And this was the real mark of the champion. Someone who could experience fatigue, emotion, pain and yet, stay calm: some of them could even smile through it.

This is what I want to teach you in this book. How to go through the challenge of emotional and physical separation, which is probably as excruciating as all those rowing races, but not lose your inner smile. You will need to learn how to separate the real drama from the emotional one. To practice rationality as superior to emotionality, even if it is just for the period of the letting go.

I take people to Nepal and in our relatively simple treks this whole experience of learning to put mind over emotion plays out for every client at some time on the journey. As we journey further into the mountains, people are confronted by the distance from the telephone and therefore contact with their children, or they have to face the difference between how they expected themselves to be at high altitude versus actuality. As people face these challenges they are asked to let go, to release their expectations, their normal contact with the children, their fears, their ambitions, because the mountains are bigger than our ego. The metaphor is perfect for our journey in letting go in relationships.

You will see that there is a lower mind, a middle mind and a higher mind in your body. We will deal with each one separately. The lower mind is the one that wants to win the rowing championship so much, but it is also the one that gives up, half way. We can't be led by our lower mind – material attachments. Our middle mind is the mind that can become overwhelmed with panic; it can throw in the towel purely out of humiliation or be 100% inspired if it smells victory. The higher mind just goes from the start to the finish, with love and inspiration, win or loose the higher mind is committed to the experience of the journey, rather than the outcome. All three operating in harmony are a formidable team.

I recommend reading this book three times. On the first reading and when you complete the three exercises in the back of the book, you'll have a firm grasp of your current reality. On the second reading you'll start to see the future in a new light. On the third reading you will be fearless and therefore ready for the next intimate relationship. You will be healed without the cost of time. You'll be amazed at how each time, at different stages of your emotional journey, different parts of the book will have completely different relevance to you.

I wish you happy, inspired and guided reading,

Live with Spirit

Chris Walker

Learning to Let Go is Learning to Love

Nobody can teach you how to love. It's as natural as taking a breath, but people get asthma, or live in places where the air is thin, and so, sometimes things get in the way. So, clearing the path to that natural love which exists inside you is something you can always improve.

What reveals the quality of our love and the depth of our blockages more than any other experience is our capacity to let go. Yes, that's right, letting go is the greatest testimony to the quality of your love. Let's explore that idea for a moment.

The opposite to love is emotion, all emotion. So even happiness, fun, generosity, and kindness are not love; they are emotions. We so often mistake the nice feelings of positive emotion for love and in doing so get trapped holding onto relationships that are finished, thinking that it is love that holds us bound to our partner.

But love is never attached. The classic story of the man holding the bird in his hand who turns to his friend and claims "look at my beautiful bird", which prompts his friend to suggest "open your palm, and see what happens." The bird flew away and the guy was really pissed, "you made me lose my beautiful bird" to which his friend replied, "anything you have to hold onto is not yours, it is only trapped. When you open your palm, you find the truth, it flew away, so it was never yours to begin with."

Love is never afraid of loss. When you love someone you will encourage them to be themselves. You can't claim to love someone and be controlling or possessive. Those are negative emotions that come from fear, not love. Your partner needs to come to you because they love you, not because you made rules or hooked them with your games, tricks or threats.

I have seen wealthy men withdraw child support for their dependent children because they say, "I love her and I don't want to lose her." Can you imagine a more stupid mathematics; acting like a clown in order to prove their love? I have also witnessed people spying on their partner to test their integrity. When relationships gravitate to this level of poverty, it is truly time to move on.

In the name of love, people abuse each other, control, cheat, lie, manipulate and hold on in the worst possible situation. But here's the rub. The more you hold on, the less you love and the more you hold on, the more you push your beloved away. The man who gripped the bird could hold tighter and tighter until he crushed the spirit from this delicate animal. This is not love – this is poverty.

In Nepal and India I have lived with people who have no money at all, but none of them are poor. They have wealth because they have love and they trust it. They trust love more than anything. Even in the face of great challenge they trust love. This is their God, a trust in love.

There is not a clear boundary between love and emotion. It is not black and white, but they are two different topics. Emotion is romance, seduction, sexuality, manifestation, creativity, birth, life and death. Emotion is everything except love.

Instead of the black and white lines between love and emotion, you might consider higher and lower emotion. The higher emotions are approaching the boundary to love while the lower emotions are a far distance from it.

Lower emotions include: anger, fear, control, sadness, jealousy, lust, attachment, guilt, infatuation and resentment.

Higher emotions include: detachment, kindness, gentleness, care, compassion, and appreciation.

The path between lower emotion and higher emotion is gratitude. The more gratitude you can have for who a person is, and who they are, the higher the emotions approximate toward love.

Even if you are in a healthy relationship letting go is important because a relationship that is built on attachment is unsustainable. Attachment comes from the absence of love, and a relationship without love is a contract of arrangement. Such things fulfil goals but the human spirit cannot live without love. Contracts of arrangement, like marriages without love (attachment) can only exist with affairs and deception.

The art of letting go is therefore a vital skill whether you are moving to a new arrangement with your partner (separation) or wanting to celebrate more love in your current relationship. Moving your emotions to love is the key to healthy relationship no matter what the circumstance. This is the art of letting go.

There are many layers to love. According to the ancient Laws of Nature, there are 7 layers that can be clearly defined. In this book, I have grouped them into 3 categories: The lower, the middle and the higher mind love. The lower and middle levels of love are really emotions. They are responsible for romance, sexuality, safety, security and your expectations for the future. These lower and middle levels are where we get attached.

Higher mind love is true love. Emotions of the lower and middle minds are mistaken for love, although they are important ingredients of relationships. Emotions are the trigger for seduction, attraction, sensuality, and commitment. They have their role in relationship, but they are not love. Emotions are what we mistake for love, and therefore justify our attachments.

So, when you are 'breaking up' it is these lower and middle minds that hurt. Emotions are fickle and this is a recurring theme in this book. Understanding the value of emotions on one hand and learning never to trust them on the other hand is the great wisdom of the ages. Emotions are the source of all pleasure and the source of all pain. You can't have one without the other. The more you trust the uppers, the more you experience the downers.

In the greatest study of all human nature, the ancient teachings preceded all religions and understood that the way to control people is to control their emotion. Those teachings demonstrated that attraction and repulsion are two sides of one emotional coin; you can't have one without the other. Infatuation entering a relationship guarantees resentment on the way out of it.

The manipulation of human emotion has become the domain of marketing, religion, politics, the media and relationship. This has benefits and drawbacks but it is not love. Love doesn't posses. If you can learn to love, you can 'let go' and become wise to the games of marketing, politics and media at the same time. Remember, the more you let go, the longer your relationships will last and the happier you'll be during separation.

They are one in the same topic. People, who are good at relationship, are also good at letting go. Controlling, fearful and lower emotional people in relationship, apply the same mechanisms to letting go, and suffer.

Conclusion

Learning to love is learning to let go. The skills of being in a relationship with love are the same skills for letting go. To understand this we separate the human condition into lower, middle and higher minded thinking. The energy for love comes from the higher mind, while the energy for romance, seduction and intimacy comes from the different levels of the lower and middle mind. These are separated into lower and higher emotions. Lower emotions grip and can't let go, these are the focus of much of this book.

Breaking Up is Easy if You Know How...

The classical belief about breaking up is that it is, and should be painful. Given the accepted models of how to break up, and the social belief systems around relationships, I can accept that for most people, it is hard. But it doesn't need to be.

I'd like to propose a process for breaking up where:

1. We don't focus or trust our emotional reactions to people, while at the same time, we don't ignore those emotions.
2. We don't accuse people of behaviours that are independent of our behaviour. In other words we empower ourselves to modify both our own actions and our partners reaction in breaking up.
3. We get completion, faster, cleaner and with less drama.
4. We can move on without the requisite years of 'getting over' the last relationship.

My personal insight is to stop the funding of unnecessary lawyers, therapists and others who prey on the apparent misery of people who are unable to let go. I'll demonstrate in these next few chapters, using steps one, two and three, how you can flush the toxins from your system, come to an emotional and authentic completion with someone and therefore prevent the heartbreaking drama that is so often a part of letting go.

The one word I want you to remember throughout this entire journey is 'respect'. Respect for yourself, your partner and the emotions that seem real, but aren't. Really, love is never attached, so in dealing with emotional drama and pain in break up we are never dealing with the issue of love. It is a big mistake to think such a thing. We are only ever dealing with our thoughts, emotions, fears and guilt. This is the really important point. Love is not attached. Emotions are, and emotions are not love.

Breaking convention – Finding the real path through breaking up.

In a recent consultation with a client who was going through the drama of separation – again – they mentioned something about their journey that I believe we should know more about. It is a very helpful insight.

When scientists talk about separation they speak about the four phases of it: Denial, anger, sadness and acceptance. The study of grief is a very thorough one. They claim that when we lose something we must go through those four cycles, over and over again until the time frame between the first and the last comes down to a few minutes. In the beginning, that time frame was several weeks or more.

My client expressed some vacillation between some of those phases. However, because their 'separation' was voluntary, the vacillation resulted in the experience of wanting to go back, and then wanting not to go back. Unlike a death or loss, there was no finality to it. This lack of finality can cause huge problems in concentration, happiness, health, focus at work and lead to a minor depression.

The scientists don't really have the whole story; and with a better understanding of 'letting go' we can better understand 'holding on' as well.

As we established in the previous chapter, we have three minds. Lower – body impulse, Middle – emotional impulse, and Higher – meaning pure impulse.

When we think about someone, especially in the case of holding onto them (attraction) and or letting go of them (grief) we rarely vacillate within one of those mind impulses. We actually vacillate between minds.

The lower mind might feel loss because of our sexual need, our physical attraction or even our sense of security that we get from that person. So, on one level the mind is thinking "I can't live without them" – this primal and essential nature can't change, but it can change who it focuses on. So, we might say we can't lose this dependency, only transfer it to another person. This is why it changes in time. We find another source to fulfil our physical need.

The middle mind on the other hand is more logical. It rationalizes the circumstances and says, "look, here's the good news, here's the bad news, which one are you going to listen to". This rationality results in feelings called emotion and it is this rationality that can change over time. In the beginning we can say, "oh, they are so perfect" but over time we might say, "Not so perfect, a few flaws." As we do this shift in rationality, our emotions of attachment go away.

The higher mind doesn't give a damn. It just looks on with amusement. So, when we tap this level of our being, which we do with amazing regularity, we don't have any feeling at all. They are not gone, and they are not here. We don't need them, and really don't miss them. Now, we tap this higher mind 1000 times a day. For most people that's an accident of life. They just go to that space in the course of everyday life listening to a song, writing an email, having an orgasm, eating cake, watching a movie. We go to this space with amazing frequency. Most people can't control this 'going to their higher mind' so, when they do, it doesn't last long.

Healing is the ability to get these three minds sorted out. It doesn't take more than an hour but most of my clients report a huge guilt at being able to walk away from someone without remorse or sadness. So, every time their higher mind lets go, they feel bad because it is heartless, and drop back into one of the lower minds, attached or emotional.

This up and down cycling is what scientists mistakenly refer to as the grief cycle. They are really right in seeing the different phases, but wrong in thinking that they are essential in grief. They are only essential when we are clumsy and primal in our process of grief.

Instead of this we can break up without heartbreak and emotional drama using the following steps:

Step 1. Have respect for your lower minded attachments. You have needs like, security, safety, health, protection, and sexuality and this complex web of personal foundation needs to be held sacred. If you lose the source of this security you must replace it fast transferring the needs somewhere else.

Step 2. Have respect for your emotional experience without empowering it. Here you can be honest with yourself about the pain of breaking up while at the same time, remaining sane. Your heart and emotions are important, but they are not the whole story.

Step 3. Learn to have respect for your higher mind. Don't empower healers, guides, Gods other than to direct you to what you already have within you, and that is love. No matter what you do, and above all else, you need to keep this truth at the forefront of your journey through letting go.

Step 1 - Learning to Let Go - Detachment - Transference of the Lower Mind

Recapping: There are three minds involved in letting go. The lower mind is the physical experience and we need to re-attach this to others, i.e. transfer it away from our source of attachment. Then there's the middle mind, which is rational, emotional and logical. Finally, there's the higher mind. In this chapter I am discussing the detachment process for the lower mind.

Nearly 90% of our pain in separation comes through the attachments of the lower mind. Physical need. But please don't be fooled. Physical does not just mean sexual. It means so much more.

Physical need includes: security, safety, warmth, future happiness, financial, career, and even a spiritual sense of place in the world. You can see that physical attachment to someone is very complex because it captures so much of our unconscious communication with ourselves and with others.

Our physical attractions encapsulate our need for mothering, fathering, care, kindness, acceptance, and feeling wanted in the world. So, we tie many subconscious agendas to the people we are attracted to. Now, the fact that these ties are subconscious is the real trauma because it means we don't know they exist. We can only presume they exist. For example: a child who is 'diminished and put down' might grow into an adult who seeks sexual activity with many partners. They transfer their inbuilt and well-hidden need for love (from their childhood journey) into the acceptance they get from an intimate engagement with a lover.

The Buddha said something like "the best way to clean mud from water is to leave it alone. The mud eventually settles to the bottom of the bucket" He even grew lotus flowers out of that mud. So, trying to purify ourselves by eliminating these subconscious attachments might be akin to stirring up the mud all the time. Goodness knows there are billions of these tiny threads of association lodged in our brain.

Osho claimed that the best way to eliminate those physical attachments is to take anything we seem to be attached to, and overdo it. His teachings were that if we are getting subconscious needs met through sex, then this is really distracting because we get highly attached to anyone we are sexually attracted to. So, his remedy for this corruption to our real capacity to love was to over do it.

He taught his students who had sexual issues of attachment to their lover, to go have as much sex with as many people in as many circumstances (always safe sex) as possible. The idea was that eventually the benefit of the sex would wear off. The same thing is taught in chocolate factories where employees 'eat the profit' – in some factories they actually encourage employees to gluttonize themselves on chocolate, knowing that once you overdo the eating to the point of sickness, you'd never eat chocolate again.

I've met both the Buddha-following students who prefer to say "it is what it is – leave it alone" and the other groups who either 'do it till they drop' or analyse themselves in order to process their 'baggage' – in my observation, none work authentically.

All those paths are subject to delusions. The indulgent one seems happy but always fearful that someone else might take their 'source' of pleasure away, so they tend to be insecure around love. The 'out of mind, out of sight' group, are so vulnerable to the uncertainty of the future, they become controlling and obsessive. The processing group who are always following a philosophy, trying to fit their real nature down the barrel of some prescribed 'goodness' are always nice people sitting on a powder keg of defensiveness and anger.

The lower mind can only love what it posses, so, the most unconscious attachments come from this mind. The lower mind is the source of great passion and attraction but it is never satisfied. It gathers, and then gathers some more, then some more and some more. It sets goals greater than last year, even if those goals are meaningless. It must have a 'next.' Hence, it reached for someone it loves, then after capturing them with seduction it becomes discontent. That's why the honeymoon usually doesn't last. Lower minded attractions always need – something or someone else. They are unsustainable.

If we could master this lower mind and all the complexity of its attachments, it's psychological profile, its subconscious links between what we want and what we are holding onto, we'd solve 90% of the world's problems – especially in domestic relationships.

The mechanics of the lower mind in natural law are that it is the source of primal attraction, birds and bees stuff but it is only the beginning. Animals often stop at this lower minded level and simply move on after copulation, dogs and cats for example. But humans and some animals have a middle mind, and therefore they are capable of emotional and mental attachments. The lower mind is meant to seed the process but it cannot sustain it. Relationships need higher levels in order to sustain health.

Addictions come from this lower mind. In relationship, people become 'addicted' to their lover, rather than in love. Remembering that love has no attachment, so, we can't say "my pain in letting you go is because I love you so much" That's a lie.

Here are a few thoughts that might help provoke insight if you are one person who finds it hard to let go:

Love and the attachments of the lower mind are two different things. If you love someone or something, you know you don't own it. The greatest love in fact, is letting go. To be detached is to love. Many people are socially conditioned to own everything they love including other people and their children as a way to control what they believe is the object of their 'love' – but this is just lower minded attachment.

You only want what you haven't got. So, attachment means that this person you are attached to has something you need or want. But you have everything, you are everything, so it's just that you think their 'bundle' is better than your 'bundle' – that's a lie, it is self corruption.

They are 'the one'. Every time you fall in love, you'll think 'they are the one' but after some years you might see someone in the street and think, "oh no, maybe they are the one". There is no 'one.' When we are looking for the 'one' we are really searching for a lost parent, a relationship that never completed. And that relationship – with the parent – was actually leading us to the real one, ourselves. Thinking someone else will be 'the one' is like fishing for sharks with a pin on a cotton thread.

Resistance to change. We love change, as long as nothing changes. We change our undies or socks, we change our hairdresser, but changing our beliefs – now that's another story. We change our country, our job, our house, even change our hair colour, as long as our beliefs don't change we seem to be ok. So, sometimes what holds us stuck in attachment is not love, is not wanting to change. We're stuck with something we don't like, and given the chance we'd change them too, as long as we don't have to change our beliefs. Now that's not right, is it?

Projection. There's always a deeper meaning. We hang on to the current reality primarily because we are getting something that is hidden from view; something that we haven't been able to identify with. So we might be attached but can't explain it because it's deeper than logic. Sometimes we use words like "there's just a special something", or, "we are just so perfect together" this is really masking. Underneath the attachment to another person lies a shark with big teeth lurking in the shadows of the deep. So, really, we are not happy with them but we are not happy without them. Revealing that there's something else going on. That's where I help people.

Association for self-importance. Sometimes being with someone who is beautiful, clever, famous, attractive, smart, wealthy rubs off and makes us feel important too. Especially when we feel a bit small in the world during uncertain times. When our tail isn't up, and we're feeling frail or not as important as we'd like to be, we associate. That means suck the lifeblood out of someone else in order to sustain ours. This association, in my experience, accounts for over half of all the 'addictions' to past relationships.

Circumstances. The real issue with addiction is the cost of it, which I believe to be more to do with your circumstances than anything else. Let's say a woman meets a man and she becomes infatuated (addicted) to him. They break up and we monitor her journey through the drama. If she has money in the bank, confidence in the future, a good solid home, a health program for her fitness and some sort of personal spiritual practice she will still experience the pain, no escaping that, but for how long and what would her reaction be to the break-up? This is what changes with circumstance. Now, take the same woman and empty her bank account, reduce her confidence in the future, an unstable home, no fitness program and a materialized form of spiritual practice like alcohol or food, in other words no solidarity for her spirit, we would see her experience the break up totally differently. She'd certainly be 'more attached' to her lover. She'd say 'but he's the perfect one'.

Power. In every consultation regarding a relationship break up, there's the dumpee and the dumper. The dumpee is always in the most pain because they lost their power. Of course, according to the Laws of Nature, the dumpee, (the one who got dumped) is usually the cause of the dumping. (Nobody does to us more than we do to ourselves) - so actually the dumpee usually sabotaged the relationship because they wanted out. However, no matter who caused the dumping, the one with the least power in the matter of separation seems to feel that they have been made a victim. In that one experience of becoming the victim there is more pain than most people can handle, so, people cling on to avoid that pain. They don't really want the relationship; they just don't want the pain.

Solutions to the lower mind attachments in relationship.

Self Discipline

You'll hear about all sorts of psycho therapeutic and spiritual mumbo jumbo that might or might not help you in love. But the one guaranteed way is discipline. It might not be the easy way. It might not be the most pleasant way. It might at times not be the most romantic and sexy way, but it is always the fastest and most accurate. Lower minded attachments in relationships are a problem, whether we are breaking up or getting into a relationship. Have the inner strength and integrity to communicate with kindness – always. Have the self-respect to know the difference between love and intimacy. Have the wisdom to sustain love but not get attached. Have the confidence in nature to know that all your fears, worries, reactions and uncertainties, will pass in time if you just don't react and weaken your resolve.

Integration

You have to become what you love in them. Take what you are attracted to in their personality and become it. Learn the art of integration. If they are creative, express your creativity. If they are strong, experience your strength. Nothing is missing it just changes in form.

Power

Empower yourself, be the cause of the break up, no matter how it looks. Know that no body does anything to you that you are not doing to yourself. In this way you can't be a victim. You might feel like they dumped you, but you must know that nobody does to you more than you do to yourself. So, if they left, and they dumped you, they were just doing what you really wanted to do to them. In this light nobody dumps you, you actually wanted them to go, to get out of your life, but didn't know how to do it.

Discern

Learn the difference between love and attachment. Learn that love is detached. Love releases people. Imagine that each person you know has a garden surrounding them as they walk, it moves with them. You can't see it, but they can. You step on a weed but it could be a flower. So, to discern between love and attachment stay outside this fence don't think you have the right to stomp in other people's garden. That's not love.

Transference

One lady was very attached to her ex partner. I first taught her how to love a man she didn't like. She thought that she had to like people, agree with them, feel attracted to them in order to love them, but that is a bad idea because then the world shrinks and we start to block love. Learning to love people whether she liked them or not was an important skill. Then I taught her to become whatever she admired in him. She did this and felt great. Then I asked her to determine the real cause of the break-up and why she manifested it. Last I asked her to witness how she had already, or was in the process of transferring all her affections and relationship needs to others. She invented some new ones like playing the piano and going for a jog and eventually she found nothing was missing. She still had love for him but there was nothing he had that she didn't already have. She separated her lower minded needs and attachments from him and could unconditionally love him. That's how we learn to let go on the lower mind level.

Step 2 - Balancing Your Middle Mind - How to Heal Your Emotional Heart

We've discussed the essential transference of emotional attachments in dealing with the lower mind and its desire to 'hang onto' people, places and things. It has little more awareness than an animal, highly instinctual, protecting itself, creating safety and security, whatever that happens to look like.

We agreed that the lower mind can't go away, but instead, we simply transfer the attachments it has from one person to another person or to self in order to heal.

A key ingredient of that is the ability to 'un-heal' when the job is done. What do I mean? There are an incredible number of people who get shut down to love and intimacy because they heal themselves through transference of everything they depended on others for, to themselves. They become independent – individualized – and therefore egocentric and self-sufficient. Hence they remain primarily single, forever shopping, never buying.

So, to 'un-heal' ourselves, and bring completion to the letting go cycle, we need to focus on cause and effect, the middle mind, our beliefs and emotions.

Do you remember pushing a child on a swing? You pushed them; they went up and out and then back to you. This is emotion. The push for emotional swings is your beliefs. If you get good news, according to your beliefs you push, if you get bad news the swing comes back. It's also like the see saw in a children's play park. One side goes up, emotions are high, and then the other side goes up, emotions are low. This is the indisputable middle mind world of emotion and beliefs.

In separation, or heartbreak, the see saw is really out of control. Up and down and up and down. The more up it was, attracted in the first place – the more down it will go, resentful in the end. Emotions are essential in life because without them, we couldn't experience life. But they are fickle. They have no base in reality. If you think you are right your emotions go up. If you think you are wrong, your emotions go down. Right and wrong have no foundation except in your mind. This is a fiction that can cause enormous pleasure and enormous pain. It's all made up. The miracle is to see through the fiction of your emotion. Here's how:

For every door that closes another is spontaneously open. So, if you lose your wallet out that door, another wallet appears at another door. If you lose your relationship out one door, another relationship is spontaneously appearing at another door. Nothing is missing. Nature abhors a vacuum. This is the masterstroke of detachment.

You might think that you are losing something. But you can't lose something; you can only lose your expectations. If your expectations are broken, in other words, if someone does something that you didn't expect; then you call it a broken heart. They love you, admire you and respect you, but they left you. So you might say they broke your heart, but really, the only thing they did was to not stay around – like you expected. Your expectations got broken, not your heart.

People can block your expectations – they cannot block your love. So, our expectations get rejected. This is the journey of the middle mind. To release the expectations and therefore, the pain, if someone leaves, why not say "I didn't expect them to stay forever" – that's wiser than moaning about a broken heart and feeling sorry for yourself, isn't it?

When going through a break-up it becomes very easy to infatuate the person and the relationship you had with them. I have seen people go from absolute disinterest in a partner all the way to being suicidal without them, just because they are breaking up with them. The best way to avoid this pitfall is to apply the Laws of Nature number one: "There are two sides to everyone and everything." Never forget it.

When we are in a relationship we might see all the bad news. When we are out of a relationship we might see all the good news. The reality is the mix of both and they are perfectly balanced. Absolutely.

When I go to my second home in the Himalayas of Nepal, I am lucky because I get to spend time with monks who live in monasteries and nunneries way up in the mountains. Once I asked "how do you deal with all the pretty women who come marching through here, looking for approval?" The monk who has become a good friend said, "We are taught that desire is poison to our meditation so if we feel this desire we simply acknowledge that we are only seeing half the person. If they look beautiful to our heart and our eyes, then we simply imagine their colon filled with waste, which all people have, and that levels them out into real humans. We simply try to love people for their visible and invisible qualities. We know there is duality, we just need to imagine it and the desire is gone."

So middle mind pain, heartache in break-up comes from the perception that there's something great about our ex partner that is not balanced by something not great. It is the emotion that comes from an imbalanced thinking process, which is in direct conflict with universal law. All is dual, everyone has good and bad. Really, this is the trigger for all this emotion and ultimately that illusion takes some people to suicide. They die because they think something bad can happen without something good. Or they think their partner is suddenly perfect, even when only two days before this, they were complaining and criticizing them.

Separation causes us to become endarkened. If we were resentful before we broke up, we will be infatuated after. The thing we need most is the belief, the trust in the law of nature that unravels this emotional illusion. The law of balance is the law of trust.

When my marriage failed my wife said, "Chris, I love you but don't trust you and I can't live with a man I don't trust" – I replied, ambitiously trying to ignore the reality "but I won't do it again". She was well coached by her therapist "my trust will never come back" and she was right. You can live with someone you don't love, even an arranged marriage, but you can't live with someone you can't trust. Trust is the real foundation of relationship. Once lost, forever lost.

But the greatest trust is self-trust. The only real question is which self do we trust. Do we trust the lower minded self, with all its attachments? Do we trust the middle minded self with all its lopsided emotions? My suggestion is that self-trust does not come from trusting yourself. It comes from trusting the laws that run your life. Something greater than the 'self' – and rather than trust a humanized religion, I suggest the universal Laws of Nature are the foundation of incredible trust. They never fail, and don't change from country to country and they do not have any vindictive motive. The universal Laws of Nature evolve everything equally, including you.

The Laws of Nature also help to empower you by making you the cause of your situation instead of the dumpee you become the dumper. You cause your situation and therefore you can get the idea that deep down you really want to move on and let go, it's just that you don't quite trust that things will be better in the future. This is the trust I speak about for you.

Knowing that there are two sides to everything is just the beginning. Once you know it you have to become it. You have to apply it, by trusting your life on it. This is why we suggest you go out into nature and explore the Laws of Nature. You have to experiment for yourself because until you trust the laws as your own, they are just blab, blab, filling your head with intellect.

Don't trust your emotions or your attachments, they are fickle, and in the ancient teachings these are the real 'devil' – it was never a fire or nasty bloke beneath the surface of earth, nor is it a place you go after death. Hell, the devil is your lower mind and purgatory is your middle mind. It's all just nature's law and made into frightening myth to scare people.

With trust, your will can kick in and start to support you. But if you apply will without trust in something higher than yourself you will always feel insecure, vulnerable. And this is not going to work, because it is trying to force yourself to change when you really don't want to.

With trust in the Laws of Nature, you trust something bigger than yourself and this is the power of the higher mind because then you just hold the trust, and automatically your willpower will take a whole new position. Higher will and your will become the same, and you begin to work hand in hand with nature – universal law.

With Will – there is integrity. With will emotions will not always rise and suffocate you and block real love. With willpower we are like trees and we can let the emotions be like leaves in the wind. If we use our willpower to overcome our cravings we break addictions, so willpower is the most powerful self-help program because it's the power your already posses. All you need is a trust in a power greater than yourself. The universal Laws of Nature are exactly that power.

When you are feeling the pain of love it is attachment of the lower and middle minds. Here's how to rise out of that pain without causing more.

Follow the guidance

I believe that we are guided in life. I believe from the Laws of Nature that there are no accidents and that everything is meant to be as it is. I think that we create an idea of where we think we are going, or who we are going to be with next week, but this is not always how it is. We create ideas that are straight paths between point A and point B, but the path is not always straight. Nature never moves in straight lines, only our expectations do.

Life is a miracle, but only if we can see that the circumstances of our day are perfect and that they are actually guiding us. We think life is hard if our mind goes hard, fixed on ideas, unable to adjust. If you are driving a car and it breaks down, don't curse it; ask yourself where you are being guided.

Life is a miracle if you can find the circumstances of your life as part of a beautiful story, if you can learn how to reinvent yourself whenever information conflicts with your expectations. Which one are you going to trust, your ideas or the universal laws? This is the real question and I am suggesting that, by looking for the miracle in your relationship break-up you will find the gift sooner than later. Then you can flow with change.

We carry a picture of our lives in our mind, our heart and our emotions. That picture is of our own invention and it is important. All our hopes and dreams are bundled into expectations and goals for the future. Sometimes we get it perfect and we project that picture of ourselves out into the world and attract the people, places, objects and things to make it real. And sometimes we get it wrong, we project our expectations out there and life just doesn't go as we wished. It is in these latter circumstances that we must reinvent ourselves, and change our expectations. As a monk once said, "I don't understand the west, you always want what you haven't got. We find it better to want what we've got. Then there's no suffering.

If we get stuck with a picture of the future that includes a person who is not appropriate or who is no longer available, we need to let it go and create a new picture; one that has a whole different set of characters.

The characters in our self-made movie, i.e. the pictures of our future, are real, but they are not irreplaceable. Take a man with a wife but she dies. He might say 'the future is a disaster' but he is wrong. The 'wife character' in his movie can be replaced, in fact nature will guarantee it but he may not be able to let go the past, and so, the new relationship is blind to him. He can't see it because of his attachment to his now deceased wife. But he can love his deceased wife and move on in hours if he knows how. It is not a crime to heal fast, but it is important to heal well. His wife was not a particular person; it was a character in his play. He doesn't need to change the script, just the actor.

Sometimes our life movies are built around certain characters and therefore they become parasitic. For example, a woman might meet a man who is very demanding of her, but the fact that she now has some assets she didn't have before: like a boat he owns, his royal family in London or a really big budget for luxury gives her the idea that he'd make a great partner. Her movie gets written off and her life becomes dependent on a specific person but this is a really difficult situation to sustain. Two people can share a vision, two people can have independent overlapping visions, but there is no health in a relationship where one dominates the other.

People in desperate situations grab onto relationships in order to stop themselves from sliding down the dark hole of despair. They reach and grab and hold on. But then, as they climb out of that dark hole, they ask, "do I really love this person?" And the answer is often, grateful yes, but love them, no.

Changing your mind means seeing things differently. To do this, it is wise to see the Laws of Nature playing out in every step. See the miracle of guidance and love in your life. See that you can't lose anyone you love; you just might lose control of them. You are never without. Nature provides. There is never a vacuum of anything in your life even if it feels like it, nature is supporting you and providing you with everything, just in a different form to what you want or expected. The faster you can change your expectations to fit the reality, the faster you move on.

This is what happens naturally with time. Time heals all wounds. Time gives us the benefit of hindsight. But we don't want to wait for time to heal what we can heal, do we? If we can work in harmony with nature, we can accelerate the healing. In fact, healing takes no time at all. Only the ego and the lower mind take time. Real healing is instantaneous. If somebody leaves or passes, you can come directly to the higher mind and love them and leave them. It's not difficult but we are conditioned to make it difficult. I hope this section of the book has helped break through that conditioning.

Beyond conventional mumbo jumbo

In determining how to heal a broken heart my experience has been that too much emphasis is placed on the psychology of it all and not enough placed on the real guidance we are getting from nature. We are always guided by nature: Everything that happens in our life has nature's hand in it. If we can see and feel that guidance, our break-up has meaning, it is just a process of adaptation and focussing on the real issues of our life: like lost vision and desperate circumstances.

Step 3 - Moving It All to the Higher Mind - Rising Out of Pain and Suffering

Higher-minded love is beyond the mechanics of relationship and the tampering that comes from emotion, in other words it is beyond attachment. It doesn't own the person it loves. It loves. It doesn't need to change the person it loves, it loves regardless. It doesn't control, because love is not about control or fear or other lower minded necessities. Love is. That's it.

The best way to learn the difference between love and emotional attachment (the thing people call love) is to do a demonstration. Take a cup, fill it with water, go to the sink and empty it, turn it upside down. What is left in that metaphorical cup is love. The cup may look empty, but you know it is not; it is filled with things – air – you just can't see. The water that filled the cup is emotion and thoughts and achievements and things materialized.

The empty cup is often the very thing we fear. We fear empty because we can't hold it, or buy it or sell it, or touch it. We can't control emptiness and so, people think it is not love. They think that anything they can't see is really nothing. But love can't be seen, just like the stuff in the empty cup, you can't see or touch love, you can only know love, and this is the closest definition we have to the experience of the higher mind, emptiness. We come from nothing, and we go to nothing. So, love is really emptiness: not a good or a bad feeling, just is.

All the feelings we have around love, and the romance and gifts we share are not love, they are our attempt to express love. They are how we try to express love but love is really emptiness.

Love is emptiness, and that is the experience of falling in love. Emptiness, lost. Sometimes we get so afraid of this emptiness we panic. We try to control the one we love or trick them or manipulate them. It is not our fault. We are in love and there is nothing we can do except attempt to materialize it. We try, we emote, we write poetry, but nothing can really express love. Nothing.

Stillness.

I sat on a mountaintop, in Nepal, and the wind blew through my veins. I was lost, completely open, confused. And when I got used to this state, I found enlightenment.

I ran to meditation, and bent my body in yoga. I found health, I found control but I lost my enlightenment.

The real meditation is life itself and the formulae to that meditation are the laws that govern all. If we see order in chaos, if we see beauty everywhere, then we are enlightened. The challenge is to see beauty when we have emotion.

To be wise and enlightened in life is very easy. We just need to run away from struggle. We can stay single and righteous. We can stay wealthy and untouchable. We can be aggressive and violent; this is how the small person achieves the enlightenment of their life. They limit their emotional exposure by controlling their universe. This prison is no heaven. This is enlightenment at the cost of someone else. Sitting on a mountaintop, enlightenment is easy.

I want to share with you the tools to become enlightened during your struggles and in the midst of real life. This skill is called stillness. You can use the laws that govern life in order to understand life, and what we understand we can love.

During challenge like separations and letting go we become 'darkened' because our emotions become so strong that we feel 'small' and 'overwhelmed' and this is what we need to reverse in the enlightened stage of letting go: we must prioritise our higher mind and know how to go there at will.

The emptiness is stillness, the stillness is emptiness. And this is the place in which we are merged with our soul. We are home, out of our mind, free. Love. But reaching for enlightenment or stillness is like reaching out to snatch smoke out of the air. The harder you try the more you push it away. Instead you must let it come to you.

Stillness begins with your body. Can you freeze your body, lying on the floor for 10 minutes, without movement? That's willpower too, absolute denial of sensory habits. If you can do this, not move a muscle for 10 minutes, you have made great progress in your life.

If you can freeze your body sitting in stillness or lying in stillness, you are learning how to feel the enlightenment that sits behind the drama of lower minded emotion. This is a powerful beginning in the process of letting go.

Now, you can progress to the middle mind. Learning to focus your mind on one topic is the next step. If you can hold your mind on one thought, for 1 minute, you have progressed remarkably. There is only one way to master this level of stillness and that is to do what you love and love what you do. To find a sport or hobby or passion or occupation that you love and do it with all your heart and soul, to devote time to it that is pure and uninterrupted.

Many people work for money. Many people do sport to compete. Many people do art for attention. But the real inspired people work also because they love it. They compete because they love it. And their art is their real creative heart, they love it.

When a person does what they love they lose track of time. They lose track of what the world thinks. They must not be interrupted because it breaks their chain of thought and those thoughts are in the zone, perfect stillness. Their body might be moving around a stage or in an office but their breathing is minor, their eyes are not flickering, the phone isn't ringing. To them the whole of life is in this one moment. This is the stillness of the middle mind, putting your heart into something.

Do what you love and love what you do.

When you do what you love and love what you do, you are in your higher mind. And this is the absolute completion of letting go.

Much of the reason for break-up is caused because we put our heart into someone, instead of something. When we lose our middle mind passion for our work or our sport or our hobby or art, we turn to a lover in the hope of bridging over the vacuum. This is a sure guarantee to cause relationships to fail, a guarantee that the relationship will not last. And it make the break-up twenty times more painful than it needs to be because it is not the relationship that is the problem, the greater story is we are self suiciding. We lost our passion or vision, for life and turned it in on a relationship instead.

Nature did not create human relationships as a means to their own end. She created human relationships to help people do what their passion drives them to do, to inspire people to do what they love and love what they do. But people turn relationships into the filler. They fill the space for doing great things with their life with a person and that kills the relationship, eventually.

When I first got married at the age of 19, I had passion for everything. It was easy then, because the whole world was an invitation to go make the best of it and my wife and I shared an amazing journey of asset building, child making, travelling, educating ourselves, sport achievements and much more. It was great for 7 or 8 years until we started to achieve all the dreams.

Now we had a family. Now we were wealthy enough not to worry about money. Now we had achieved sporting success, and we'd travelled and all the dreams of our youth had come true. My business was successful and even though there were many challenges the youthful enthusiasm had been replaced by mature maintenance. My spirit, my inspiration, my vision for life desperately needed a kick in the butt, but I was too 'made' to solidify in my ego.

I started seeking different forms of inspiration. Changing my sport, buying new homes, taking risks in business, investing, and taking the family on great holidays. Really, the whole thing was a self-indulgent panic attack. I was no longer inspired and I was certainly not doing what I loved and loving what I did. Down and down I went, grasping at more and more short-term things that could re energize my spirit. I didn't even know something was wrong.

In retrospection, I needed to do a vision quest. I needed to re inspire myself. But I didn't get it, so I turned in on myself becoming more and more self-absorbed. Drinking more, flying around the world on business trips, making business deals that were unfair: milking so much out of each situation, trying desperately to grasp any victory.

It led to a series of affairs. Places I felt young and inspired again. Of course, it was also grasping at straws. There is no relationship on earth that can compensate for lost passion. I was off my path but didn't know it. The choice was grab anything or sink in some malaise – possibly depression or alcoholism, or chronic fatigue or cancer. I grabbed with my fighting spirit but it was like a man in the ocean grabbing at fish to stay afloat, nothing lasted more than a few weeks, 6 months at the most.

When we get ourselves lost, we are the last person we need to ask for directions. And we know it. But if we are lost and don't know it, then we are a danger to everyone. I was lost, but, like 90% of people going through a relationship break-up, I didn't know it. I didn't know that it was my lost inspiration – passion – for life that was the issue. I thought it was my relationship.

Nature destroys anything that does not fulfil its purpose. And relationships that block a person from giving their inspiration to the world around them, are part of that destruction (cancer is a last ditch resort to get people back into their inspiration) – So, holding on in relationship is usually exaggerated far beyond its real issue. The real problem is that one or both people have lost their youthful passion for life, and gone into maintenance, survival.

The most important skill in learning stillness, and therefore mastery of the middle mind – is to do what you love and love what you do. To find a passion, outside a relationship with a purpose, social contribution, creative outlet, or sport; and do it with all your heart and soul, obsessively.

The idea that needs to be taken into consideration is that there are many elements to life: Work, money, health, relationship, children, society, spirituality, global events. And they must all achieve a level of devotion. But there is something, which sits over the top of all these and this, is your inspiration, your passion, and your purpose in life. It is like a silk thread that weaves its way through everything you do. The passion to animate life comes from this. The musician builds their life around their music. The artist builds their life around their art. The writers around their writing, the race car drivers around car racing and; everything fits around it, including their relationship. Never be ashamed of your passion but never use it to avoid your lower mind responsibility to yourself, your family or your world. They can all work in harmony. See my book Personal Harmony.

Your vision of the future – Magnetism.

Love has no logic, so this muddy water is thick with emotion. Don't let anyone make up your mind for you, but at the same time, don't act impulsively. The key is to know that it is going to be ok, no matter which way it goes.

Love itself doesn't lead to attachment. So, the ability to love someone, and the process of letting go are very much the same thing. Ultimately all pain in separation has nothing to do with love. It has to do with fears, needs and most importantly, our future dreams.

When we are going through personal crisis – like our career or family, we overly cling to relationships. This often smoothers them and leads to their collapse because we loaded too much of our emotional baggage onto someone else. Our partner is not our therapist, psychologist, business coach, doctor or lawyer but often we treat them as if they are. We seek all sorts of things from our relationships during times of challenge and therefore sabotage them. So, sometimes, when our work or health is at its worst we cling so hard to someone, we actually place excessive pressure on our relationship and blow it away. So, an important step in sorting out whether to stay or go is getting the rest of our life together.

However, the real issue regarding the question of stay or go is the future. Any relationship with great sex and good food can be made to survive the present moment, however, the real magnetism is the proposition of the future. When we lose trust for someone, we lose trust for the future so we start valuing the moment. All we want is present moment happiness because anything else is just impossible to even image. This relationship is over.

When we fulfil all the goals we ever dreamed of, and can't create an exciting challenge for our future, our relationship is over then too. People grow apart, and when we lose the inspiration for the future it is because we've retired from life, 50 years too early. Our relationship has become our nesting place and love has been lost in the ambition for safety. This relationship is also over.

When our partner says, "it is over" then it is over. We must learn when to be hopeful and when to be honest with ourselves. Being disrespected when our partner is too busy, stressed, worried, messed up, lying or dishonest is a good sign that it's time to move on. It's like owning a house that no one can live in. The relationship is dead but there are two people still sharing a house.

There are many different ways people leave relationships but still stay in them because they don't want to fail or because of the kids or money issues. People can emotionally abandon their partner but stay in the structure of the relationship, 'just for the kids' or they can transfer their passion elsewhere. Workaholic, stressed, excess travel, substance abuse, obesity are often signs that this person has lost what nature provides in love, and is searching for it everywhere else. To be the partner of such a person on a long term basis is really challenging.

There are also many people who stay in relationships because they fear change. They prefer a non-emotional, comfortable and safe home than the uncertainty of the singles market so they stay, and complain. These 'convenient' relationships are complex but if the individual understands their choices, the real motive for staying then there can be peace and harmony in that home.

In healthy relationships there is a strong need for two people to share some common dreams of the future. Many relationship problems come when two people merge for different objectives. One person might want sexuality, intimacy and romance; the other might want children, home management and financial stability. While both get those specific needs met then there will be an ongoing, but somewhat complex attraction. But there's always a tension.

Alignment between the goals, ambitions and future plans for couples is very important. However, this is not just about cars, boats and houses. It includes inner emotional satisfactions and notions of lifestyle.

Our inside world is motivated by different things to the outside world. Our outer world is easy to understand. It wants more happiness, less unhappiness. That's the lower and middle minds competing for supremacy in a world of material things. So, if we are some place where there's discomfort, the lower minds want to fix it, adapt to it, or run away from it. This is called 'buying the new house', making the 'new baby', going to sex therapy and all else. However, the inside world, the higher mind, is motivated by something vastly different.

So relationships often come to an end even though two people love each other. They end because the future becomes uncertain and the relationship becomes uncertain with it. There is no compromise here. We are either on the path that inspires our future, or off it. When we are off track, no relationship will work. When we are on track, any relationship with love will work.

What is vital to remember is that you can't get inside someone else's head. You can't change people. Once they disconnect their future from you, then everything you do, other than to wish them happiness is futile.

Another way you can determine how long a relationship will last is to ask each person about the future. The soul speaks in pictures so, I often ask people to describe their mental picture of the future. The number of times they say "I" reveals their level of self-obsession and therefore, their real motive for being in a relationship.

Still on the same question, another group of people will reply with "they" meaning that their vision of the future is for their children, partner, parents, friends to have a good future. This is self-obsession turned inside out and reveals that their real motive for being in a relationship is, like the first example, themselves. These people give to get. They soon burn out.

When a person sees the future in terms of what they want for themselves or others they have positioned their relationship as a mechanism improving their circumstance and these people will be bitterly disappointed. Eventually their hopes will dry up and their nice affection will turn to frustration because if things aren't perfect now, they are certainly not going to get better with time. Even money doesn't make people happier. These people complain that they never get what they deserve.

Doing a vision quest with your partner is the best way to determine if it is over or not. In my book, 'Sacred Love, The Honeymoon that Lasts Forever', there's a vision quest for lovers that can be done over a few weeks. You do it independently and then come together with the maps of your futures later. It details the process of checking whether there is a real vision and then creating a shared vision of the future. A couple that can share a vision for the future are inseparable, their souls are talking, as well as their bodies. When people don't have a vision, desperation and self-obsession brings them to relationships with very immediate needs. Money, support, pleasure; these relationships go up and down like a brides nightie and is very unstable.

Understanding Relationships Using The Laws of Nature

When I was a child my Dad used to tease people of other nationalities and religions. It was an Australian cultural game, and everyone had a nickname. Most of these nicknames were not complimentary. Australia still had the 'white Australia' policy and those immigrants that had managed to enter the country were teased relentlessly.

When we don't know a lot about something, we fear it. It is on this basis that we become fragile in relationships, because what we don't understand we condemn. In learning how to let go, one of the more significant contributions to a smooth path is the wisdom gained through the insight gained in nature.

We come from nature, we are born in nature, we live connected to nature and we die into nature. City people are different in Nature. They are happier, friendlier, more generous, and more compassionate in nature. People dream more and live more authentically when they are close to the earth and, in contrast, all our pain and suffering comes from our disconnection from the Laws of Nature.

We need to nurture and cherish this connection to nature, our livelihood and our love for our family is housed in our attitude to nature. What we abuse in nature we can abuse in our homes. Yet, it is clumsy to run into the bush every time we feel stressed or out of balance. We are city people and we have centralized services in cities to bring us all to a productive harmony. Now, the laws that make living in nature so perfect are yours to take wherever you go. This way you are always connected. We call this Self Mastery. Now, even from the comfort of your armchair you can revisit the tranquillity, inspiration and heart opening beauty of nature, anytime you choose.

The Laws of Nature are ancient. They've been studied and taught and passed from teacher to student for thousands of years. Now they are yours if you are ready. To live in this world with higher consciousness is a profound step out of the mass of the mundane and into the unique realm of inspiration: a place in which love, stillness and personal authenticity thrive.

The Laws of Nature are above conditioning, reaction and confusion. They are simple and pure to the degree that we can be honest with ourselves, cut the rhetoric and separate our emotions from our truth. It is the degree to which we can live authentically and in peace with life. This is the essence of letting go.

The cost of separating ourselves from nature is being recognized not only in the environmental cost, but also in the human cost. The personal cost of separating people from what is true and natural is becoming unbearable, romance and relationships are suffering.

Nature's Way – Healing the hurt of love.

If you are hurting or have been hurt by love, then you are simply out of harmony with nature's law. I have studied many ways to live and I have studied many ways to heal a heart. Each has their own magic but none are as powerful as the simplest way of all: Nature's way.

So you can check that you are living in harmony with those 'natural laws' and where there is a 'break' you can understand the source of your pain and fix it.

The first step in healing is a diagnostic one. Find out where you are in conflict with natural law. Nature does not want you in pain. It wants you to be healthy, challenged and happy. So, your pain is a conflict with nature, let's see where, then go fix it and get you back on track.

The Law of Balance.

All of nature is created perfectly but sometimes it doesn't seem that way. A flood or a fire might wipe out a lot of land, animals and some people. But for every flood in one part of the earth there is a drought somewhere else. For every Tsunami, there is a perfect calm somewhere else. But human emotions cannot see this balance, human emotions see only half stories: pain without pleasure, etc.

Sometimes when we love people, we are blind to this balance. We think they are either all great, or all bad. Very rarely do we actually see that all people have human nature, and therefore all people have balance, two sides. In classic romance people present to us the good side of themselves, or that's all we want to see. But after you know people for a while you'll see the reverse everything you think about them, and then you can see both sides of them. This is real human nature and real Love.

Most of our pain in life comes from the broken expectation that we found an aberration to nature's first law. We get such a surprise that someone we love has two sides. We loved them for only one side. We saw all their good and we totally loved that part, however, we lost our connection to nature, we started thinking with our imagination and became blind to their whole self. The pain we have is that we thought this person was half and then they turned out to be double sided, whole. It is not their fault; in fact they are perfect. They just presented the parts of themselves you wouldn't judge as bad. So the real issue is how much of the world you judge. They just presented the bits you wouldn't judge.

Nature is balanced; everything is either in balance, or seeking it. Love is not blind but our emotions and feelings are sometimes blind because emotions want to see half worlds, half people. They want good without bad, peace without war - Delusions and illusions. So, the pain of love is sometimes a chance to see both sides of someone and really learn to love them; and to unlearn our judgements and become wiser.

To heal this conflict with nature we must learn to expand our mind and see beauty in both the dark and the light instead of foolishly and emotionally seeking half-truth.

The Law of Evolution.

Sometimes our pain in love comes because people change. In nature nothing is permanent it is always evolving. There are many people who think that it is wrong for nature to change; they fight for the status quo and try to stop the rainforests from change, or specie from becoming extinct, but they can't stop nature. It has been on a path of change for 3 billion years. It is not going to stop now and human progress is a part of that evolutionary process.

Our pain in love can come because we thought that our relationship was going to be the same forever. We got disconnected from the reality of impermanence and created a mental dream that who we met was going to be who we lived with for the rest of our lives. In that disconnection from nature's law we really attract a lot of suffering because love is never static. To really turn up in your relationships, you need to remember that love starts like a seed but must grow into a tree. It cannot just survive feeding on itself or stay in the same form. People's needs and expectations are at their least when you first meet them. However, that's just the seed. One satisfied need leads to another and eventually tests the capacity of the relationship to expand.

Nature destroys anything that doesn't grow. So, when we fix our mind on an idea, an expectation that is fixed, unable to expand, then we get a large pain when nature destroys our attachment.

Impermanence and human expectations are the difference between reality and fantasy. Only those things that stay in growth will stay together. You can explain most relationship heart breaks because two people came together to achieve a goal, not a purpose. They came together in love, completed their mission together and grew apart. The holding on is the cause of the pain, not the coming together in the first place.

The Law of Interconnectedness.

In nature all things are inter-connected nothing is ever missing. However, humans are individualized into yours and mine. It is this individualisation that causes unhealthy dependencies that are in direct conflict with natural law.

If you melt a block of ice you get water. If you heat the water you get vapour. If you super heat the vapour you get steam. If you capture the steam and cool it down, you get a block of ice. The water molecules changed their level of excitement, but the molecules, atoms and sub atomic particles stayed the same.

Now this might seem like worlds away from any sort of relevance to relationships, but it explains so much about human nature. We think we are separate from other people like we are vapour and they are ice. But really we are all the same, just in different levels of 'excitement.' When we separate ourselves in this way we see different cultures, different sexes, different beliefs and different races and therefore define the world by what we have and what they have or have not got. We become blind to the fact that we are all connected. We get possessive and define ourselves by our knowledge, beauty, wealth or religion.

Those things do differentiate us, but they are not permanent and only important to our ego mind. If we transport those differences into love and relationships we become competitive, possessive, fearful and protective. We loose the ability to surrender and be thankful. You see nobody is missing anything. They have it all, just in different forms.

A common cause of love pain is this loss of awareness of our interconnectedness with other human beings because we start thinking of ourselves as independent individuals. That in turn means that we treat others as independent individuals. Now, our connections to our real nature, to the nature of life are broken and are replaced by self-obsession, self-interest and judgement.

You see, our conflicts with others and with the broader world are based on our desire to protect our individuality. We start splitting the world around us including our partner, into categories of good and bad, strong and weak, pleasure and pain. This is understandable but the problem comes when we become rigid in these definitions. Ultimately they lead to the conclusion that there are lovable parts and unlovable parts of our loved one and if we are unwilling to change our judgements, we'll try to change them. And this is where we get dumped.

When we divide people into lovable and not lovable bits we start wanting to fix people. We break the inter-connection of our real nature to the Laws of Nature. We fragment and start telling people what's wrong with them, telling them why our judgements are best, and then our head begins to rule our heart. That is often why there is pain when relationships break up. It is not a broken heart; it is, in fact, a broken set of expectations. We start wanting to change people to fit our fragmented view of the world; into lovable on our side and unlovable on the other side; and in doing so, belittle people. This is what finally blocks our love and what we must heal.

It requires a little faith, but if you look hard enough, people actually are mirrors of you. They might not have your car, or your bank account, but they have their ways and they have their wealths. They have everything you have but in different forms. So, actually, when you learn to love others for who they are, you are learning to love yourself. And that's the root of the pain of a broken heart. The love you were projecting onto them was really meant for yourself, and now they look like you; you just can't share it.

People are not individuals after all. In human nature, you and your partner are just mirrors of each other. What you like in them is just what you like in you, what you judge in them is just what you judge in you. It was easy to put these higher and lower aspects of yourself into other people rather than witness them in you, but it is false. Nature won't allow it.

If they lie to you, you lie to you; if they are attractive, you are attractive. If they are successful you are successful. If they are beautiful or handsome, so are you. When you remove the separations of the ego, instead of seeing other people as individuals that you love or don't love, see the world of human nature as the perfect reflection of your own human nature.

If you love someone, really love them, then all you are experiencing is the love you can have for yourself, and all humanity. Everyone in the world has every human trait. There are no individuals, just personalities that display 'lovable bits' and hide 'unlovable' – the fact is, all human traits are lovable, even if we don't like them.

This awareness eases the pain of love because you realize you are just looking in the mirror. Nature wants you to accept what you see, not split it, or create a fake personality. Your human nature is worthy of love and for everything you like about yourself and others, there's going to be a balance side. Both need to have your affection. They are all part of the magical experience of love. You are what you see.

Thankfulness and unhappiness cannot exist in the same heart. What you appreciate grows, what you can't appreciate depreciates. Wanting to help, fix, change, modify, support, challenge another person is in fact a conflict with nature, you are being unthankful for who they already are and ignoring the fact that you only judge in others what you judge in yourself. This triggers the reaction that ultimately ends in a broken heart. If you can learn to appreciate others you can appreciate yourself. If you are always trying to fix people, especially if they don't ask for this help, you are actually running yourself down too.

The Law of Harmony.

The pain of love can also be described as a lack of harmony in our heart.

In nature there is a rhythm, and that rhythm is harmonious. The cycle of birth, life and death is the rhythm of nature's harmony. When we resist this cycle we get heartbroken.

The cycles happen hourly, daily, weekly, monthly and yearly. Like the tides of the ocean, or the seasons and years, there are cycles within cycles. To survive those cycles we must learn a constancy that does not ebb and flow.

A tree grows toward the sun. That is constancy, but then a house might shade the sun or another tree might block the rays, so, the tree bends in order to adapt. There's a constancy of intent, with a flexibility of process. Many people can't flex, they are rigid in their ways, and in contrast to this many people follow their emotions as if they were the sun. Neither is healthy and both extremes make it hard to live in partnership with that person.

The rigid person thinks a cycle is permanent and allows no time for exploration. They hang on and can't let go. The emotional person never gets a grip because their whole being is focussed on themselves. Sitting in a rubber boat going down the Grand Canyon without a paddle, the emotional person is hanging onto their identity with grim death, unable to open or surrender to love.

The more gratitude you have for people, the more harmonious you will be. The more harmonious you are the more harmony there is in the world. So, rising from middle mind to higher minded thinking requires appreciation. Thank the world and the world will thank you. Appreciate your partner and they will rise to meet you.

The Law of Hierarchy.

In nature there is always a purpose. Anything that does not fulfil its purpose dies. The lower levels of nature feed the middle and the middle feeds the higher. Everything in nature is hierarchical. Everything has a purpose.

Your relationships have a purpose too. Sometimes we think the lower levels of mind and their gratifications are the purpose, but they are not the top of the hierarchy. They are the foundation. Sometimes we think getting what we want in our relationships is the purpose, but this is not the top of the hierarchy either.

So, we can get bewildered that what we thought was a perfectly good relationship got crushed for no good reason. But there is always a reason in nature. Anything that is not fulfilling its higher purpose, gets recycled…

Our relationships break so either one or both people can move on in their life. We hang onto love because it gives us a sense of belonging, and this is wonderful. However, it is not always possible to hang onto the source of that love. We may be required to let go the person, but hold onto the love. It may be time to move higher in our own hierarchy of life.

Staying Sane During Emotional Turmoil

"All human problems come from our inability to sit quietly in a room by ourselves" - Pascal

During challenge, when your emotions overwhelm you, it is vital that you find the courage to hold discipline. Most personal catastrophes happen during emotional challenges when people react and do things they regret.

When emotional turmoil comes, and you don't know what to do with your relationship, or how to release it, then it means you are stuck. This is very dangerous. There are plenty of excuses and justifications to keep you stuck in your emotional and mental thinking. So, you have to get away from that.

You need nature. Go for a swim, climb a safe tree, take a walk in the jungle. Whatever it is, don't take your prison with you and set fire to everyone else's house. Let it go and let your mind focus on whatever it is you are doing right now.

As either a mental game or on paper start listing all the things you can be thankful for both with and without your partner. List them till you go green. You can't be unhappy and thankful at the same time. The more thankful you are for all the things that are going on, the more power you'll have to feel good about yourself. This is completeness and important for dealing with emotional turmoil.

Spin the story, tricking your lower mind.

If you can't let go it could be because your mind has attached something positive to this person and this positive thing is more important than letting them go. We create stories that are not exactly true and in doing so get ourselves locked, unable to let go. We spin stories that trick our mind into thinking that we can't live happily without someone, or that without them our life will never be as good. This is rubbish and the Laws of Nature reveal it. As said before, there are two sides to everything but our emotions only know one of those two. So, we get to think all is good news even when there's evidence that contradicts it.

Be mindful – don't give in.

It's tempting to let emotions overwhelm us and think that our reactions are going to fix things, like drinking alcohol or taking drugs when we are emotionally down. But those things always lead to journeys that are unnecessary. During your emotional downers, don't be easy on yourself. That's just reinforcing the belief pattern that caused the problem in the first place.

During challenge create routines. Create processes so that if you feel bad, go sit alone and feel bad for a while, set the alarm clock for half an hour, wallow in the misery, let the pain come in, go inside and do its work and then, when the alarm goes off, shake yourself out of it and refuse to go back in until later today when you schedule another 'wallow period.'

Denial of feelings just protracts pain but giving those feelings complete reign over your life is self-sabotaging. If you feel a surge of emotional overwhelm, then cut yourself some space and time, tell your boss you need a few minutes and go immerse yourself. Holding on just means you make yourself and everyone around you miserable. Go let nature do its thing, and then when the alarm goes off, come out of it, fighting.

The periods of immersion might be frequent at first. Maybe every 2 or 3 hours you need to wallow and maybe you need someone to help you so that you can really let yourself experience the pain but after a time they become less frequent until they stop.

During emotional crisis don't tell everyone your sad story. It just reinforces the illusion that your emotions are real. However, at the same time, give yourself some time and space to accept the experience of the downer: the worst thing you can do is to try to pretend nothing is wrong.

If you pretend nothing is wrong and swallow your feelings then it is like a pressure cooker and the pressure builds inside you, sending all the toxins into your muscle tissue. Eventually it becomes chemically bound to you and cause illness.

In emotional downers, you can even go for a jog. Your physical body needs health during emotional times because emotions are chemicals that you need to keep liquid in your body, and eventually flush. Drink loads of water, no alcohol, avoid starchy food and sugars that acidify you. Alkalize your body with anti oxidants, green vegetables and umaboshi plums.

Unfinished business that gets in the way.

Unfinished business between two people can give them an excuse to remain in some form of complex relationship for years, even if they are physically separated.

The mummy – daddy role attachments are pollution to relationships and can account for significant problems in letting go. The attachment formed through these unconscious bonds dig deep into the adult psyche. Adults believe they are not affected by their childhood, but as Freud said "give me the child before three and I'll give you the adult"

We are born with the emotional baggage of our mother and father as chemicals within our body. As soon as we enter the world we start reacting to that baggage and the environment and by the time we are three, it's concrete.

Our unfinished business is the source of the greatest and most difficult attachments because it drags itself along behind us and suffocates our love. We either wrestle for control or act like children in relationships and, it is on this basis that so much unseen emotional attachment surfaces when it's time to let go.

If you or your partner have any unfinished business with your parents, whether they are alive or dead; deal with it. If you still feel that your childhood was not perfect then process it. If you feel that you can be a better parent than the ones you had, then it's time to grow up so that you can turn up in a relationship. This is tough talk but it is honest talk. Anyone who is still angry, judgemental, righteous, or infatuated ("they were so fantastic") with anyone from their past, can't turn up in their current reality.

When there is a lot of emotion around letting go, it is rarely love that is the cause: it is usually because we are letting go of the parent we never had. We often project onto partners all the hopes and dreams of your lost childhood and they are the adult version of the parent we never had. It might be wiser to learn how to give ourselves this care, rather than attach it to another person.

Emotional self-management during crisis.

During emotional crisis, keep your spirits high. Lifting your spirit is not something you should worry about night and day but, when things are overwhelming, this self-focus is very important. It shouldn't need to last more than a few weeks.

1. Be compassionate and kind to yourself.

2. Don't react to anything. Spontaneous decisions in emotional states of mind are unwise.

3. Exercise a lot.

4. Go into the bush. Find inspiration in nature.

5. Balance your opinions until they are ambivalent.

6. Listen to music that you love.

7. Spend time with friends that you love.

8. Be thankful.

9. Start planning a bright new future without this partner.

Take Time Out

Downtime, or recovery time needs to be efficient and short so we don't spend the greater portion of our personal time recovering from the stress taken up during the active part of our lives.

There are some really important skills needed to ensure the quality of downtime. They include, but aren't limited to:

Active relaxation
Emotional clearing
Spirit (inspiration) regeneration
Youthful play
Self-Awareness
A regenerative activity

There are many reasons why balanced time fails to regenerate energy:

A nagging dissatisfied partner
The use of alcohol or drugs to calm the nerves
Too long a time between uptime and downtime.
Television as a means of relaxation
Extreme stress in the uptime mode
Lack of fun in the downtime activity
Emotional drama that carries over
Lack of metabolic increase during downtime (flushing)
Excess eating, sleeping or partying.
The inability to break away from the problems of the uptime life.

A deep, pervasive emotion (anger, resentment or hate) for something in uptime.

Regenerative rest – means faster balance…

1. Don't wait too long

The longest period between balancing sessions should be around 4-8 hours. Those are conscious time-outs during which you: switch off, remain calm, distract your mind, stimulate your breathing, and calm your nerves.

Meditation is hailed as one of these practices. Yoga is another. However there are hundreds of ways. What you must be careful of is to make sure you avoid any of the following in that list; eating, drinking, sleeping, talking, doing nothing, slow walking. These are the classic, half measures in balance. They don't work.

2. Do learn mind control techniques that achieve:

Emotional clearing, inner calm, rest, refreshment of the brain, breathing techniques, focus and re-inspiration. We teach these in seminars, not in books.

3. Don't do nothing

Putting your feet up on the desk might feel relaxing but if you are, for example, dehydrated before rest, and then you'll be dehydrated after it. You need active rest techniques that really cause recovery. These are taught in most meditation classes, yoga classes and others. You might find them challenging at first, so, the benefits might take a week or two to flow. But they will flow and make your rest, active.

4. Don't include your relationship in the downtime management cycle

Your partner does not want you to turn up in their life for the purpose of downtime. You might think that your relationship is part of your downtime space but it is absolutely not. In your relationship there are uptime and downtime spaces. So, be very careful.

I have seen more relationships struggle because of this one thing than all the rest put together. If your uptime management is so challenged that home is the only downtime space you give yourself, then your relationships will fail. You'll be trying to please yourself (take time out) please your partner (give them enjoyment) and recover from your stress (active rest). These are three competing forces. Incompatible.

5. Do get outdoors

Recovery is nearly automatic in nature. In a park, a garden, a forest, on the ocean, near a river, the list goes on. However, you have to be doing something. Take a photo, throw a Frisbee, play football, skip a rope. Just taking a basket of food and some wine out into nature is fantastic but don't include that in your balance downtime. Include it in your relationship uptime.

Conclusions

Everything needs to be fed. If you don't feed something it dies. So, you obviously know that you need to feed your work. You also know that you have to feed your relationship. If you have children you know that you have to 'put in' with them in order to give them healthy emotional nurturing. So, there's the feed out. Now, what are you going to do to feed the source? If you feed your work, your relationship, your children, your family, your friends, your body, your mind – how are you going to balance all the output?

We've mentioned that waiting more than four hours is a killer. Some people wait a week and say 'boy I am looking forward to the weekend' – and even worse, other people say 'only 6 months till my annual leave, I just can't wait' – That's disaster in the waiting because in the meantime that person will use their relationship, their children and their health as a means of downtime relaxation. That's sucking the blood out of things that we need to be investing energy in.

So, learn to balance your life on the run. Learn the skills of putting back what you put out. Don't do it with food, parties, TV or sleep. Do it with active rest, positive mind clearing, fun and most important – get outdoors, actively.

Stress Management – a Key to Personal Change

Crazy? Anxious? Worried a lot? The cause of so many calamities in relationship is often stress. Stress should be a sign that we, not the world, need to change our mind. However, for most people stress is a sign that the whole universe screwed up and that they should change their job, their partner, their therapist, their religion. This is upside down. Stress is a sign that we are blocked, not the world around us.

Stress is like a prison. Here we are trapped behind bars, shaking the cage, screaming and shouting for someone to let us out. But the bars are in our head. The loss of harmony comes because an individual thinks their thoughts and beliefs are right, and the world including nature, got it wrong. This is a profoundly stupid idea but the most common human error on earth. Trusting our emotions.

There's a thousand ways to redecorate the prison too. I have a client who came to me 5 years ago. I couldn't get through to her then and I told her so. She hated her ex-husband so much because he was a 'controlling' entrepreneur. This lady went into this relationship with a stressed out needy man, playing the sweet nurturing woman and enjoying the vast fruits of his wealth. Of course she was giving nurturing to get it and after a year started to complain that he wasn't giving her what she wanted. He demanded she stay on the same terms as the relationship started because his stress was so bad, without her he was messed up. She moved on physically but five years later she was still running her victim script.

In the meantime she'd joined Scientology and found that he was a PPS, a potential problem source. Now she had found an institution to validate her prison. He was a problem source. She was fine. She stuck at that, like most people for a few years then wisely moved on. Now she followed Madonna into "The Kabala" – another reinforcement that he was the bad guy and she was the victim. Her prison stayed firm, but now it was redecorated with her Jewish friends, a sort of victims club.

Stress is a sign that we have a prison and the key to unlocking those bars is to unlearn life, not learn some philosophy. Philosophies like Scientology and Kabala are the prison: along with Buddhist teachings, Hindu, Christian and Moslem. They separate us; keep us locked into judgement. Their purpose, in control of the lower minded energies is perfect but their function in healing, really learning to love is contradictory. Nature will teach you, those boundaries; those ideologies are the entire ego mind. Few of them bring people to love.

Grow from stress.

Many people back off from life when nature is telling them to put their foot on the gas. The new age fortune-teller might say "oh, it's stressful, turn away" and you shouldn't pay for that advice.

Stress is a gift. How else do we know when we've peaked? Human consciousness is an ever-evolving thing and stress shows where it's stuck. It's the radar.

There are many options we have when we get stressed or overwhelmed or anxious. Most of them involve backing off in some way. But you can be sure that all backing off process lead to cancer. Breast cancer, prostate cancer, lung cancer, money cancer, love cancer.

Nature doesn't listen to our complaints, so why should we? Nature says, "Evolve or die" this is really clear. It is the core inspiration of nature, evolve or die. So, stress shows that we are prepared to grow, to challenge the box we put ourselves in.

Many people shy away from stress claiming that it is a measure of their lack of consciousness. But no, they are being unconscious by seeking peace, they are self sabotaging. In a relationship, if you want stress free time you'll need to stay single or have a sex mate, as is the current trend. In a real relationship you can have stress free time for a while, however, it doesn't last: it isn't meant to. Love grows at the border of chaos and order.

If there's no challenge in your relationship, you're dead. If there's too much challenge in your relationship, then there's too much pleasure too. Sometimes people even leave a relationship when the challenge goes out but really, they are complaining that the pleasure went out. This is the lower mind at it's absolute best; seeking pleasure without pain; seeking support without challenge. Emotional stupidity.

Some people leave relationships because the pleasure goes out. But they fail to recognize that the pain went out too. When we find the middle path in a relationship both pleasure and pain moderate. What it means is, we can focus on other priorities.

Great relationships are distracting. Not just because they are pleasure but also because they are painful, chaos and order are always balanced. Support and challenge are always balanced in love; so to the busy stressed entrepreneur or performer, a great relationship might be one filled with love, but not too high on the pleasure pain spectrum.

But stressed people seek antidotes. So they seek pleasure-full relationships to counterbalance their stressful business life. They are totally living and motivated by their lower mind because this is where stress takes us. Stress drags us down into our lower material mind. It makes us horny or celibate, it makes us attached or rejecting, it makes us needy one minute and independent the next. A see saw of emotion.

Affairs and quick fix sex are the result of repetitive stress. People get stuck in mortgages, obligations, jobs they can't leave and then they are also stuck in their head, they can't change their beliefs so, the only outlet is 'pleasure only' flings. These work but the downside is that if life is nature, and nature grows at the border of chaos and order or support and challenge, then the more pleasure we get outside the home, the more pain we get inside it. People fail to see the nature of things and therefore throw petrol on a fire thinking they are going to extinguish it. Stress doesn't get relieved through pleasure.

Repetitive stress injury.

The same stress over and over is like a dog biting you 20 times as you go through the gate, 20 times. It's the most important witnessing. Is the same stress hampering your life, year after year? If so, you've built a nice prison and it might be time to unlearn the thoughts that built it. More pleasure is not going to fix stress.

So, stress is a gift. A real gift but only if you grow through it. To grow through stress means you think differently about the same situation, rather than change the situation. That means, you learn how to do what was stressing you before, without stress now.

Here's an example: (it's about time you say!) – Let's pretend I speak for a living. I stand up in front of audiences and talk. I get paid for it, so, there's an expectation from the audience that it's entertaining. So, let's just say that my self-imposed stress limit is 20 people. I can almost do that and keep my underwear clean.

Now, I get a booking for 200 people. Just the thought of it makes me tremble. I can self-sabotage, which most people do, "oh, I have a sore throat" or "gee, I'm busy" or I can face the music. Now, if I don't evolve, I'm facing 200 people with the same headspace I had with 20. I am totally stuffed. So, instead of that disaster, I seek help, and find a teacher or someone, or Zanax and do the talk.

If I did it with consciousness, guess what? I get a booking for 500. Damn, I thought it was over, I thought I was clever, but now I am dumb again. I have to go to a teacher again. But I can't go to that same teacher. He/she was perfect to get me from 20 to 200 but they're hopeless at 500 people audiences. So, not only do I face new stress, I face new learning's, new teachers, and new teachings.

If you fall in love for the first time there are, in the first weeks and months, just a few issues (like my audiences) just a few things to deal with. Now, after 6 months you add the idea of living together and there are more issues, a bigger audience. Then, you add children and bank accounts and mortgages and your careers and – and – and – and. Now if your mindset stays stuck at the level it was when you first met; issues replace love. Your chaos and order sucks the life out of the romance and all your energy goes into fixing things.

What this means is that your love can't grow outside the prison walls that were built on the first day you met. The whole energy is spent trying to decorate the cell. But nature won't allow any human being to stay stuck in that cell. It brings stress to shift them. That stress is physical, emotional, financial, career, relationship, family, spiritual – in some form; nature brings stress to grow people. If the relationship doesn't evolve, heartbreak comes not because you are with the wrong person but because you built a prison of expectations and haven't grown out of it.

The Laws of Nature help you grow through stress, they dismantle the prison walls, take down the bars and let you look at your situation from the outside in. They help you evolve when you get a mosquito bite stress, and they help you when somebody dies. They help when you can't choose the brand of toothpaste and they help you when you sell your billion-dollar property portfolio. The Laws of Nature don't answer questions, they teach you how. At each level of life they teach you how to deal with the stress.

Expanding your vision is a great antidote to stress too. When your vision is the size of an ant, then ants annoy you. When your vision is the size of your ego, all things in your ego annoy you. But if your vision is big, small stuff just shoots by.

The underling cause of Stress is emotion and all emotions come from our perspective, the ways we see the world. We all have different emotional reactions based on our perspectives. If you think that life is about a relationship, then you'll have lots of emotional reactions to your relationship. If you think your life is all about money, you'll be emotional about 10cents even if you have billions. If you think life is about staying in the past, you'll have lots of emotions about saving the whales and global warming. Your perspective determines your emotion. So, if you want to change your emotion, change your perspective.

Our perspective determines the prison cell that we place ourselves in too. Religions and philosophies have small perspectives if they are fundamentalist in nature. So, those people who follow those paths react violently to small shifts in their reality. The Laws of Nature are universal. Nothing ruffles you if you can see it from a universal perspective. That's the gift of the Laws of Nature and how you can use them to keep expanding your perspectives.

Having a Great Day – Turning Up for Your Next Relationship – 15 Tips

As you begin to find the letting go more permanent, then it is wise to get your life in good order so that you can move on with health and growth.

Step 1. Today begins yesterday.

What you do today, affects tomorrow, more than anything else. So, having a fantastic day today began yesterday. Now, there's lots of ways to overcome the misdeeds and forgotten promises of yesterday. You can even take a pill or try running it off. But, eventually – compensation kills us.

Waking up to a fantastic day needs to grow out of yesterday, rather than be compensation for it. So, the rest of these steps in having a fantastic day today, also ensure you 'had a fantastic day, yesterday' and yesterday depends on the day before that. So I think you can get the drift here. Do today not what is best for today, but what is great for tomorrow.

It takes around 6 weeks to embed a new habit. Exercises are only temporary measures until habits set in. So, the other 14 steps that follow are temporary knowledge. Eventually they'll become habits.

Step 2. Sleep. The sound of silence.

I've seen people spend half their life in ashrams, running around naked on beaches in Byron Bay, bending over backwards in Yoga, chanting up a storm in a church, eating organic vegies, and fighting for human rights. All of which is their attempt to 'have a great day'

But most of them couldn't sleep well. And therefore, their day, their job, their love was always a struggle. I want you to hear this really, really, really loud. Nothing is more important to your achievements in life than the ability to do nothing.

The only thing that blocks sleep is your ego. That's not a criticism of the ego; without it we have no money, no relationship, no health, no job. So, please don't think this is ego bashing. Ego is as spiritual as everything else on earth.

But, yes, there's a 'but', the ego has to die to life. It is not the whole reality of life. If we get so confused between our ego and our spirit that we can't separate them, then stress, worry, sadness, poverty, lack of love will become a screen through which we see our day. So, the ego, at night, and several moments throughout the day as a minimum must rest.

To rest the ego is easy. Maybe that is a new habit, but right here, right here and now I'll show you how to practice that. Ready? To rest the ego you have to practice trust.

The only reason we live through our ego is to make life safe. We use it to sort of 'force' our way through life. We use our ego to 'get what we want' and if we don't use it, we end up poor, alone, and naked. Ego collects things, holds them, nurtures them, supports them and discards them when we are finished. Ego is the material world.

The only reason we 'want' is because we don't trust that it'll be 'given' to us. So, to fall asleep at night you have to 'trust' that everything is going to be fantastic. Of course, the ego never thinks things are going to be fantastic unless it is involved. It is the maker, the constructor, the thinker, and the carer. So, to fall asleep – I mean good fantastic restful sleep at the deepest level, then you have to stop wanting and trust.

If you stop wanting during the day and simply 'trust'; you'll end up on the street begging. So, there's a time and a place. To 'trust' is to rest. All religions and faiths, and spirituality try to give their followers trust. They call it faith. That's another great word for sleep quality, faith. Faith comes from the ego, but it is a restful ego that has faith.

So, that's the second step to a fantastic day. Practice 'trust' or 'faith' in order to separate your ego from your spirit. Remembering that your ego never sleeps, it can only be placated for the night.

Early to bed and early to rise is the sequence that suits the ego.

Dreams are of the ego. Dreams in the early night are unfinished ego business of the day. Dreams in the middle of the night are long term unfinished ego business. Dreams in the early morning are ambitions of the ego. And as you know, when you dream a lot, you don't feel rested. The ego didn't feel safe.

Step 3. Eat to love, not love to eat.

My chiropractor friend claims that 90% of back problems in the morning come from a full belly at night. That's just the beginning of the issue of food, rest and day-life.

Don't combine more than 5 different foods at one sitting
Don't eat within 4 hours of sleep – dry biscuits are great alternatives.
Don't eat more than the equivalent of a clenched fist (yours) of food in one sitting.
Eat 5 times a day and make sure protein is the essence of that eating.
Avoid things that quench your appetite without providing nourishment.
Eat to your lifestyle. A big breakfast might be great for a bricklayer, but an office worker will be sleeping by 11.00am with too much food for breakfast.
A big lunch needs a big rest afterward.
Something bitter, like a pickle or salad before big meals helps digestion.

Step 4. A plan.

Of all the thousands of great ideas about having a fantastic day, this next one is the most commonly used by the most successful people I have consulted to. This includes; movie starts, rock stars, business leaders, reformed drug addicts, politicians, entrepreneurs and artists. Are you ready for it?

To a person, every single successful person I have worked with has a notebook of some sort in which they plan tomorrow. Why is this so important?

Well, because people who believe they are worthy of success, and who think they are really worthy of having a fantastic day – everyday day, don't leave that up to chance.

So, for example, they have people they love working around them. They have professional people working for them. They don't work with people they dislike. So, they are always planning tomorrow so that it is filled with fabulous things to do.

In contrast I also consult to a lot of people who consider themselves losers. Nearly every single one of them has a vision plan; written down as a result of some seminar they did ten years ago. They have great dreams but a crappy reality. Of course, a few months consumed in a crappy reality is going to cause devastating ego issues and ultimately sabotage the long term.

So, back to those lists. Before you go to your bed, 'think this question' – what do I have planned for tomorrow? If the answer is 'same old same old' or 'got to solve those bloody problems' or 'I have to go and work in that crappy job' then know that you are treating yourself like a loser. You do have choice.

1. First choice is that you can find something fantastic in something terrible. That's a mind game so be careful it's not just trickery. But you can actually go to a job you don't like with a different approach that 'yuk' – you can find things to love about it, or funny parts of it. A sense of humour can cure a lot of dark thinking.

2. Second choice is that you can change it. Just know that the building blocks of a great life are great days. Miserable, 'oh same old same old' plans for tomorrow make you a 'sad sack' and people are going to treat you like you treat yourself; a punching bag for their emotional overload.

3. The third choice is that you can, in the most extreme situations drop into your spirit and trust that just because the ego doesn't see daylight, doesn't mean there isn't any. You can trust that the challenge has a deeper beauty than what you first see. Now, this is fine, but don't do it everyday – it becomes a habit of excusing all the dirt because there's a deeper meaning. You end up hating yourself.

So step four is always think ahead about tomorrow. Is it going to be a great day? And if not, what can you inject into it to make it great. It's called

'Design-A-Day'. Design your next day as something to look forward to. If you did that right yesterday then today is great, so you won't be looking to 'have a better day tomorrow'

Step 5. Don't look back.

Now that I am writing this for you, it must sound like I am doing everything I am writing. It must come across like my life is totally paradise. And I am having fantastic days. Well that is only half right.

I've got arthritic fingers from millions of hammers on this keyboard sitting in cold places writing books that no one read; and there are other things too. So, I could look back and get really pissed. So, life is a work in progress. So, in my life I have to keep processing the past in order to allow myself to turn up, and have a fantastic day today. And it's never finished. So, I don't go digging for stuff to process.

The most powerful key to having a great day is never look back and there is only one 'honest' way to achieve that. You have to be thankful for the past.

When I say 'don't look back' people turn their heads and start focussing on what they want. Their ego gets the reins and off they run thinking 'right, Walker told me not to look back so I will look ahead and keep my focus on what is coming next' – but that's not it.

Don't look back means don't have regrets. The past makes us so, if we blindside the past it might be blocked from our thoughts, but it is actually causing the present.

All the unfinished business of yesteryear is haunting us like a ghost. Buddhist call it Karma, Christians call it 'The wrath of God' – and I don't know what Jewish people call it, 'vengeance or something' and Moslems I have even less knowledge. The key is, that everyone acknowledges that what we did affects what we do.

In the Laws of Nature, the same thing, what they propose is that under the ego, there is no 'I' there is just a 'we'. So, what we do to others we do to ourselves. Like a circle of thought, what we put out, comes back. No matter how you word it, the bottom line is that 'unfinished business' from the past, corrupts our capacity to have a fantastic day today.

How you really get to 'don't look back' is that you say thanks for it. The past is spiritual. No value was ever had giving the ego control over the past. So, we need to 'trust' that the past was what was meant to be. The key to achieving that, as already proposed, is to be thankful for it.

Anything in the past that you can't be thankful for runs your life.
Anything in the past that I can't be thankful for, runs my life.
Repeat that 300 times.

And while you are repeating it, flash back to your childhood, or to a past relationship, or to a situation in your past. Think of people, places and things that were important milestones, and check, 'am I thankful' – If not, then there's sabotage in your system and the 'fantastic day' is being corrupted. Ego is holding.

Getting thankful for the past is spiritual stuff. Because the past has happened, there's nothing you can do to change it. After you go through disbelief, denial and then anger about the past experience, finally there's honesty. It happened. Then, the only course of action is the deal with it so it doesn't pollute your day.

Sometimes this needs an intervention by someone who can decipher the blessing of that past. Sometimes you can quickly do it for yourself. The acid test is 'do you fear it happening again?' if the answer is yes, it's still stuck in your ego.

To round this off, finish everyday with a thankyou for everything that happened in the day. It's the best prayer at night for kids to sit or kneel and say 'thank you for ......' instead of chanting some wish for forgiveness. Thank you, thank you, and thank you.

Step 6. Have a reason for living bigger than life itself.

For many people this sounds a bit fluffy. They like the idea of 'being happy' as the most important thing in their day. Me too. However, after a bunch of bungled attempts at that strategy I've come to a better way, one that actually works.

I found that what I get from life makes me happy for a while but what I give in life makes me inspired, content and deeply privileged. So, if I feel like what I am doing right now is good for me, I am happy, for a while. But as soon as I stop, then I need something else to make me happy. So, I think this running from happy make me – happy make me – is what causes addictions and emotional instability.

Happy make you doesn't work either because you might be a 'happy make me person' then, I am valuable for a few minutes while I make you happy, then, well if I don't keep you happy you are either sad, or bored, and what then?

I avoid branding people, but the net result of most devotion to Anthony Robins is an obsession with 'make me happy'. That idea didn't work for me, my standards are different.

However, I found that by having a sense of purpose in life and as long as I can link whatever I am doing to that purpose, I feel, content. And given than 'our purpose' is about giving to others, then it's a great model for a 'fantastic day' – link our activities to our purpose.

It gives life a bigger meaning and therefore puts things in a different context. I have met clients who are so emotionally fragile, always looking for compliments, absolutely taking everything personally. It's not because they are bad or messed up, it's because the only motive they can find for life is their own happiness.

I also have clients who work in childcare, orphanages in third world countries. These people are also fragile just like the first group, however, the fact that they have selfishly found a way to give to others and therefore find a bigger sense of their life context, they are content, happy because that giving is an awesome energy.

Now we need to be conscious here. The person, who goes out in the world seeking approval and self-happiness from their day, might just be the perfect partner. They get all day, and give all night; whereas, the aid worker or the healer might give all day and want to 'get' all night.

We must remember that there are two sides to everyone, a public and a private. Whatever a person does in extreme in public, they reverse in private. That's how you can tell those little old ladies with Victorian embroidered collars on their white shirts under their jumper going to church, are total sex maniacs when they get home!

So, back to the topic at hand, one part of us seeks to get happy; the other part of us seeks to give happy. Our ego does both because it feels good either way. The thing about giving happy is that you can turn any disaster into a victory by thinking; 'who did I just make happy?' but you can't turn a disaster into a victory by thinking, 'I'm not really unhappy'

So, learn to give in order to be happier. The best way is to measure your life by what you gave rather than what you've got. Ultimately you are going to die so what you've got 'isn't really worth anything', eventually.

Step 7. Approach. Don't attack the day ahead.

It is a sad confession that I make that I have spent the night with a few people. Yes, ok, so I've been normal. Shoot me for it! Anyways, the thankfulness of that is that I've got to witness quite a number of wake up rituals, and noticed how mine change when I woke up alone or with someone.

The bottom line is that those first few minutes when we come back to consciousness from sleep, are very, very important to our health. As a child I used to stay with my Nanna. I loved it. We would all be still up playing while dear old Nanna was already knitting in bed. She loved knitting in bed and always fell asleep with those dangerous needles and half her nights knitting unravelled on her lap. But, when the cock crowed in the mornings Nanna was already up, out in her garden getting rid of snails from the cabbages, collecting a few eggs for breakfast.

She would have set the table, made the bread, whipped the eggs and probably had a cuppa before the sun came up. Nanna died. She was 94 and she only died because someone in her family stole her money and house and broke her heart. Dear Nanna, she knew how to get up in the morning. Lucky for her that her husband died 50 years prior so there weren't many temptations to do otherwise. And from what I have heard, he was an ass anyway, so that's probably where she got the habit.

Bounce out of bed in the morning. You can do it. Then a little stretch, go make the tea, brighten your heart deliberately and if other sleepy heads are still in the bed, bring them a nice hot cuppa or something.

Step 8. Life is a miracle. See it and smile.

Now, this is a bit of unapologetic self-promotion and given the self-revelation in the last point, I can do it. The Laws of Nature are important because they let you laugh more. So learning them is important.

You see, some people don't like the news because it's always a surprise to them that the world is like it is. That is because some people think that the way want the world to be, is how it should be. This is mild depression.

Severe depression is absolute shock when the world is what it is. So, if you can read the paper, watch the news and go, 'Oh, yeah, that's the Laws of Nature at work' then what could cause depression, sadness or disappointment? Really think about it. If you know how something works then what could be a disappointment?

If I had a car, which I don't, I would know that if I don't put petrol in it, then it would conk out. If I don't put water in the water thing, then it will dry up and die. So, I know how a car works and the only thing that could be a surprise would be my own incapacity to remember such trivial matters as 'put petrol in car'

Then if I also know that too much mind noise causes forgetfulness, too much salad causes ungroundedness, too much alcohol blocks clear thinking, and worry causes us not to turn up, then when I 'forget' to put petrol in the car, I know why, and therefore don't get a surprise there either.

The Laws of Nature are universal. So, if you know a universal law, you know how everything works, even a computer if you choose to apply them. So, health, wealth, love, life, business all works on the same laws. Universal ones. Stars work on those laws too and so do cancer cells. So, you see, wisdom of this nature can be very precious.

Step 9. If you are going to do something – Enjoy it.

I live near a huge park. It's a place for people to go and do their daily exercise. What I love most is to see people doing their training and laughing at the same time. The personal trainers, who are really good at their jobs, get their little groups motivated but enjoying themselves, all at the same time. The reason is; if the clients don't enjoy their time, they won't come back.

Then there are the hardy people in the park, running and puffing and frowning. I doubt they are really doing themselves much good.

I went out with a friend last week and we had a nice meal and a glass of wine. She's a yogini and lives a really strict lifestyle but every now and then she has a wine with her lunch. It's great; she gets tipsy after half a glass. She does this lunch thing every now and then but always on a Friday, because she doesn't teach on the Saturday. Therefore, if she feels a bit off colour after the wine, she doesn't regret it the next day. She can enjoy herself.

Everything we do has a consequence and we need to build that consequence into what we are doing. A bucket of ice cream might look tempting, but, if we are going to really enjoy it, we have to accept the 'fat' and the cholesterol as a part of the fun.

That's how monks stop themselves from getting horny. They might see a beautiful woman and think 'yum' and start to 'enjoy' a forbidden fruit or at least the idea of it. So, they think of that person's colon. That's enough to bring you back to reality. They kill the temptation before it kills them.

So, when we do what we do, and we have a complete understanding of the consequence, and the consequence is fine, then, we can let go.

Grinding through work, grinding through music, grinding through the day is no way to cause this to be a fantastic day. And going to do something just because it is good for you is not enough. It must be good for you AND it must be enjoyable. Otherwise, it's killing you.

Step 10. Stand up.

Your spine is your age line. A bad spine will make you feel old even if you are young. Slouched posture, weak abdomen, slumped shoulders, short neck; head bent forward are antidotes to having a great day.

You can see how a person feels from 100 meters just by their posture. And you can feel fantastic at the worst circumstance with a good posture. There are many tools for posture correction. And these are definitely not at the gym.

Pilates, some yoga, Alexander technique, Qigong, and Tai chi are postural techniques. Lifting the inner core, holding the body well. It's amazing to see people in countries where carrying heavy loads on their shoulders in normal.

Those who are forced to do it develop slumped arched backs. Those who volunteer have beautiful straight backs. You can easily tell when a person is carrying a burden that they don't want.

And in the west, these burdens are mostly emotional. But the affect is identical. So straighten up your spine. Sit on a chair without a back rest, or one of those ball things, sit on a wooden crate it doesn't matter what, just get the habit of a straight back.

Step 11. Include challenge.

My friend often calls and tells me how hard the day has been. When I ask why, he says 'so much challenge'

Did you know that there couldn't be a challenge without a support? So, when we speak of a 'challenging day' that very same day has 'supporting day' built in. However, we go where the loudest noise takes us sometimes. So, we can easily focus on the challenge and forget the rest.

When my friend rings up and says 'I had a great day' I always ask 'so where was the challenge?' He gets totally annoyed at me, but it's true.

Wanting a day without challenge is like wanting a relationship without questions, or an apple without a pip, or a child without a complaint. It's just the way it is meant to be and if we go into these situations wishing for a 'gee don't challenge me' attitude, then we're going to be so disconnected, so unapproachable.

But more than that, we're going to be disappointed because if we want the day to be challenge free, we can't have a fantastic day. Try enjoying the challenges. It's all part of the process.

Step 12. Be certain.

If there is a myth that has been sold to millions of people it is the myth of certainty of an outcome.

It's an easy myth to sell. All you need to do is achieve and outcome and then say, you knew it was going to happen right from the start.

I've consulted to 5-6,000 people, spoken to a million, and been a part of things that involve billions. Of those people, about 20 are really where they dreamed they could be. Most are somewhere good, but this was not the childhood dream of 'I knew I'd make the top 10 one day'

Of the thousand or so athletes who make the Olympic games and the few who win gold medals millions and millions of people failed. So many were trying to get to the Olympics and win that medal. But just a few get through.

Is it because of some 'certainty' in the mind of that winner? Is it some confidence or commitment they had? Do you really think, in all honesty that the gold medal winner was the only one with absolute certainty that they would win?

Let's not do this any more. You can control the quality of your process and remain a happy person having a fantastic day. You can hold a dream in your mind and focus on all the right ingredients to win. You can practice, train, practice, train, and rehearse, and learn but, if the energy is not your turn, you might have to settle for less.

So, there is no certainty. There is only your heart, your actions and your integrity and if all these three are lined up, then the probability of success just increased. But there is no certainty, just a commitment to try.

Step 13. No excuses.

Last week I had a kidney chill. I was out in my kayak and the weather just turned and I got so cold. The next day I felt like crap. I certainly was in no mood to work. So, I got a DVD set, a warm blanket, hot tea, turned off my mobile and shut the world out. I had a fantastic day even though I felt like crap.

There's no excuse. Even someone dying is no excuse – but this requires huge spiritual awareness – so there is an excuse! 'I am not spiritually awake'

Everyday is a new day. So the sun comes up and we have a thousand justifications not to have a fantastic day. If I sit with some people I think they could win the gold medal in the Olympic excuses competition.

But that's not what they want. Neither do you. Zero tolerance means that there's always a bright side, always a gift, always something to be thankful for and there's always an opportunity to lift your spirits even when things are bad.

I saw this once in an amazing way. My Dad was so proud to teach me things. He wanted me to know how to chop wood, clear a forest, make a house, and dig a trench and concrete over the top of the garden to make it neat. So, I'd spend many compulsory hours being his Go-fa (go for this and go for that) –

Dad wanted me to enjoy work. He'd joke and laugh and tease me. The whole thing was that he entertained me, to keep my spirits up amongst the hard work. Anyway, Dad chopped the end of his finger off, sliced right through it. He smiled, wrapped a bandage and made a joke, then back to fun and enjoying the day. I fainted. Anyway, the point was, he wouldn't even let a smashed finger which needed many stitches, spoil the moment.

Really, it's got to be enjoyable. There's only one pass at this one life. Every day is so precious yet; people waste the days with excuses. Oh, it's too hot. Oh it's too cold. My goodness.

I think this was the whole message of Monty Python. Learn to laugh at it. That great song 'always look on the bright side of life' with Brain hanging from a cross. Or the skit about 'luxury' – 'when we got home, our Dad would chop us into bits, make us work 25 hours a day, sleep in a shoe box in the middle of the road, and the kids today, they just won't believe you. Ah, yes, we had it tough. Luxury'

Step 14. Step 14 is the same as step 13.

Step 15. Love it.

Just for arguments sake let's paint the world out so you can't see it anymore. There's nothing there. You are sitting here reading this long text you are alone. Now, there are about 6 trillion stars in the Milky Way. Our

Sun is one of them. And our planet goes around our Sun, just like all the other Suns have planets too.

There are 50 billion galaxies like the Milky Way. So, if you do the math, your calculator will be unable to display the numbers, it isn't built to think that big.

Now the world is still painted out. But you know it is out there. You know there are trees and birds and cars and red wine out there. So, you know. You know. You can see or know there are stars and cars and things.

This is the most important thing. To stay in awe of the magnificence of the universe and how bloody lucky we are to even know that there's sugar in our tea and taste it, let alone become conscious of the vast magnificence of it. We become a little self-obsessed.

To have a really, really fantastic day, one of the greatest gifts is simply to be excited about the fact that you're alive. Dad used to say, 'I look up the obituaries in the paper, if I'm not in it, and it's a great day'

We each need to remain so excited about life; just like a child at Christmas or Passover or whatever your faiths special day. Everyday is Christmas; everyday is your birthday, the birth of a new day. That's where great, fantastic, unbelievable days begin.

In your home, surround yourself with things from another world. Not this one. Pictures of a universe, like my screen saver from Apple. Surround yourself with amazing awe-inspiring ideas and things that make you like a child; just so ready to have a fantastic day. Like a child learn to bounce off the walls and mend the hits. Make no excuses and be like a child, smile, want life, want it to be fun. In this, you will know yourself and your heart will be open to life.

Things to Do

A process for letting go of the lower mind attachments.

What I miss in them.	Where do I have it?	Who else provides it?	What else provides it?

When we miss someone with our lower mind we think there's a vacuum in our life. But you can know that nature abhors a vacuum. There can never be anything missing in your life. It can be in a different form or from a different place, but it can't be missing. For example, your boyfriend or girlfriend might leave you. Then you might say to yourself, "I miss them" and I would ask you "what exactly do you miss?"

You could say things like "their hair, their touch, their smile, and their friendship" and I could really understand that this would keep you in pain and attached to them. But your perceptions are messed up. All your suffering is coming from an observation that is not really factual. So, why not see what getting the facts straight could do for your pain? Go on give it a try.

Say we look at the missing friendship, which is a painful thing to miss from someone you love. Now, let's see what the Laws of Nature show us. Nothing is ever missing – it just changes in form. So, someone has replaced your lost partners friendship already. It could be your parents, your neighbour, your friends, your cat, your dog, TV, your diary, your teacher or even this book. Nature abhors a vacuum so nothing is missing. We just think it is because we only have eyes for that specific form of the friendship. There's a gift waiting for you if you can just see that the friendship is not missing, it has become 1,2,3 or 50 different things. So, in fact, according to the universal Laws of Nature, nothing can go missing, it just changes form.

Now you might think the best form is the original one. Many people think like this. They say, "the best love I ever had was the first love" but they are so hanging onto the past that they just can't see the gift of the new form. Sometimes the new form is much healthier and more inspiring, less abusive.

So, nothing can ever be missing and this helps us let go of the lower mind attachments to lost relationships. We learn to let go by seeing that nature loves us. She moves the form to a different place; she never lets us go without.

A great story about this was a lady who lost her whole family in a fire. They all died, and she was left with no money, no family, no one and she thought she lost everything including her children. But she called me within hours of that event and I stepped her through the whole process I just described above. Suddenly all the physical and emotional attachments she had to her family were replaced by other people, including herself. She saw that she was not in poverty, and that her whole structure of life had been replaced in a different form. What do you think happened?

Well you will find this amazing but she felt the presence of all her lost family members. They all turned up because you can replace all the material and emotional connections but you can't and don't need to replace the love. So, grief blocks the love and when you love someone really deeply, they can't go away. They can take their body and materials elsewhere, but your love connects you to them.

So, this is a nasty example because it sounds like I trivialize the pain, but I don't: what I do is to help people cut through the fog of emotional and material attachments and find out that nature always provides us with our needs in different forms, but never replaces the greatest connection, our love for people.

When I was going through my divorce, my wife, frustrated with my ugly emotional behaviour took our three children and with her new partner sailed off on his boat around the world. I selfishly tried to stop them, but the law courts saw right through me and the judge said, "You selfish man, why would you want to stop your children having such a wonderful adventure, and with a man you considered your best friend?" She was right. That judge saw that my lower minded attachments to the kids was completely clouding my judgement. I was a total ass.

Anyways, all this is easy to look back on after 20 years, but at the time, there was such a great void in my life I could hardly imagine the next day arriving let alone survive this one. But I did survive because of what I am teaching you here.

A year later I was sitting on the beach, feeling sorry for myself, missing my kids terribly, and really still angry at my ex wife, which in itself was destroying my health, when I looked up and saw the full moon in the middle of the morning sky. I suddenly felt a relief, and then it all just woke up.

I'd really never learned how to love someone without being near them or controlling them or by helping them. I'd never thought about love for my children in any other form than contributing to their lives, and therefore getting some feedback from them into mine.

Suddenly I felt love without any condition. The foolishness of my attachments became so obvious at first I cried and then I laughed. No one can take my children away because I love them. They can go elsewhere in the physical world but never be disconnected in love.

I realized then that I'd been feeling so sorry for myself that I'd failed to see the gifts of my life as it had now become. My children were now my clients and people I helped, my contribution to them had become my contribution to other families and the warmth of new friends and studies I was doing had totally replaced the day-to-day feedback I got from my beautiful children. Nothing was missing. This is an enlightened awakening. And writing about it does no justice to the experience. You can have that experience by filling out the form in this section thoroughly.

A process for letting go of middle mind attachments.

Positive aspect.	Downside of this.	Negative aspect.	Downside of this.

Emotional Attachments come from imbalanced perceptions. I know this sounds a bit heady right now, but you will shift your emotional experience by filling out this form. The one on the page is just a model. You need at least 50 rows.

In the first column list all the things you like about this person.

In the third column all the things you dislike about this person

In the second column now find all the negative aspects of that positive in Col 1.

In the forth column now find all the positive aspects of that negative in Col 3.

You may need more space than I've provided. The key is to keep on filling out each cell until the positive aspect you once thought they had is actually seen to be a big problem too. And the negative aspect you saw in them in column 3, demonstrates remarkable benefits to you.

If you do this for everything you can think about for this person, you will no longer be attached to them at this level of your emotional awareness. Sometimes people do 300 rows of negatives and positives. Make sure that there are equal numbers of positive and negative aspects in Col 1, and Col 3. Remember, the Laws of Nature? There is perfect balance in everything.

Learn stillness.

You can bring stillness to everything if you choose to. You are healing your broken heart so, in a flash you tap your stillness and see all the pieces of the broken puzzle come into place.

The importance of stillness is that it is where your best comes from. It's a deep you and its courage is obvious. It has no fear. Inspired. No accident it's home.

To learn stillness:

First Lesson – Lower mind

First learn to still the lower mind. Lie flat on the floor, pillow under your head; arms spread out to the sides so there's breathing room under your armpits. Place a beanbag or something dark over your eyes; keep warm and no interruptions- ever. Set the alarm clock so it doesn't frighten you and start. You'll be wise to do ten minutes at a time twice a day, morning and night.

Now, the instructions, once you are lying on the floor, all prepared. Shut up. Don't move. Don't think about not moving. Don't control. Don't think about not controlling. Relax every muscle. Don't move. Not even one hair can move. Achieve 10 minutes and you are a genius. Falling asleep is ok too. No music…

Second Lesson – Middle mind

Watch the news on TV or read the paper. Everything you hear bring it to balance. If they talk about a famine, find the other side. If they talk about a plane crash find the benefit. The middle mind wants half the truth, and you want the whole truth. Everything is just an event until people judge it good or bad. So, simply judge it both good and bad equally. Cut through your emotion. Practice on the bad news and then practice finding the bad in the good news. If you can do this, you are a genius.

Third Lesson – Higher mind

Go into nature. Become obsessed with details. Look for beauty everywhere. Look for beauty in ugly. Look for beauty. Look at the disappointments and see beauty. Turn your experience in nature to one of awe. Be gob smacked. Every ant, every thing has a heart and organs and blood. Look for shapes, structures, look for the miracle. Look for this for just 10 minutes a day and your higher mind is awake. The king is on its throne. You are home. This is the experience that comes when you can dedicate your time to one thing, and one thing at a time.

When you do what you love and love what you do, you are in your higher mind. And this is the absolute completion of letting go.

Life Balance questionnaire: Are you turning up for your relationship?

The demand score

Score 10 for a 100%, 'Yes'. Score 0 for 'No'. Score from 0 - 10 for in between.

1.   Do you hate your job? Score '0 to 10'
2.   Do you have emotional conflict at work? Score '0 to 10'
3.   Do you have high conflict for your boss (can be non verbal)? Score '0 to 10'
4.   Do you have too much to do and not enough time? Score '0 to 10'
5.   Is your company going through change? Score '0 to 10'
6   Are you hoping for turnaround/change in your work? Score '0 to 10'
7.   Is your office open plan or closed private? Score '0 to 10'
8.   Do you spend more than half your working day in an office? Score '0 to 10'
9.   Do you travel by plane more than once a week? Score '0 to 10'
10.   Do you spend more than two nights a week away from home? Score '0 to 10'
11.   If you don't perform well in your job, will you be fired? Score '0 to 10'

Now add those scores......... total between 0 and 110? This is your demand score...

The balance score.

Score 10 for 100% 'Yes'.   Score 0 for 'No'. Score from 0 - 10 for in between.

1.   Are you happily single or in a really healthy, happy relationship? Score '0 to 10'
2.   Do you have any dependent children? Score '0 to 10'
3.   Are you healthy? (Weight, fitness, etc) Score '0 to 10'
4.   Do you meditate or do active rest daily? Score '0 to 10'
5.   Do you have a process to clear your negative emotion that works? Score '0 to 10'
6.   Do you get outdoors for exercise daily? Score '0 to 10'
7.   Do you drink alcohol or 'party late' less than once a week? Score '0 to 10'
8.   Are you sleeping 6-8 hrs a night without medications? Score '0 to 10'
9.   Do you watch less than 2 hours of television a day? Score '0 to 10'
10. Do you have loving friendships, partner and home life? Score '0 to 10'
11. Is your private time free from drama? Score '0 to 10'

Now add those scores ... total between 0 and 110? This is your balance score...

Score - Are you balancing your life?

Simply add the scores and see how you rate. If the differences between the two scores is greater than 30 points you need to adjust your lifestyle. If your balance score is higher than your work score, you can give more out. If your balance score is less than your work score, you're burning out. Change is essential.

* If the scores are equal you are doing good
* If the overall scores are above 75 and within 30 points of each other you are in the success zone
* If the overall scores are below 50 and within 30 points of each other you are in the comfort zone
* If the overall scores are below 30 and within 30 points of each other you probably need to get a life.

Happiness and unthankfulness
cannot exist in the same
heart.